Biking with Bismarck

Biking with Bismarck

A Little Tour of France

by Matthew Stevenson

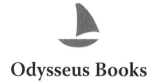

Odysseus Books

BIKING WITH BISMARCK.
Copyright©2021 by Matthew Mills Stevenson.
ISBN-13: 978-0-9970580-4-8   ISBN-10: 0-9970580-4-8   (paperback)
ISBN-13: 978-0-9970580-5-5   ISBN-10: 0-9970580-5-6   (e-book)

For fulfillment information, address:
Odysseus Books c/o Pathway Book Service,
34 Production Avenue, Keene New Hampshire 03431.
Toll free: 1-800-345-6665. Fax: 1-603-357-2073.
E-mail: pbs@pathwaybook.com

Other inquiries: Odysseus Books.
Attention: David Wogahn, publisher
publish@partnerpress.org. Tel: 1-877-735-5269.

Please visit the book's website: www.odysseusbooks.com
To contact the author on any matter, such as to arrange a
speaking engagement, please use: matthewstevenson@sunrise.ch.
Author website is: www.matthewmstevenson.com

Manufactured in the United States.
This book was printed on acid-free paper in the United States.
This paper meets the requirements of ANSI/NISO Z39.48-1992

Edited by Doreen Russo and Martin Daly.
Jacket and book design by Nanette Stevenson.
Map by Marjorie Mueller, Graymouse Graphics.

Library of Congress Cataloging-in-Publication Data
Stevenson, Matthew Mills, 1954–author.
Biking with Bismarck / by Matthew Mills Stevenson.
p. cm. (Odysseus Books)
ISBN-13: 978-0-9970580-4-8 (cloth: alk. paper)
1. Stevenson, Matthew Mills, 1954—Travel. 2. French history. I. Title.

10 9 8 7 6 5 4 3 2 1

FIRST EDITION.

This book is dedicated to my cousin,

STANISLAV STANOYEVIĆ,

*who on many occasions in our shared lives has greeted me
cheerfully in Paris and whose dedication to
human rights and French history
inspires much of my thinking.*

And to my friend of forty years,

LEWIS H. LAPHAM,

*whose passion for history, writing, and reading
supplied many of the books, and set the standards,
for these excursions.*

Contents

Foreword

THREE MONTHS AFTER MY MOTHER DIED in summer 2011, I found myself in a whirlpool of grief, a mixture of pain and random tears that was in many ways harder to bear than her death. She had not, by Dylan Thomas's formula, gone "quietly into that good night," but fought death as though it were an intruder in her house. With few medications and no tubes other than willpower, she hung on to life as an expression of determination, clearly something that she wanted to leave to her family. During some dark hour, she looked at my younger sister and said, "I live only for you."

When she died in Princeton, New Jersey, I had the warm embrace of family and friends, and I spent much of that summer with my father. Together we shared the aftermath of her loss, exchanging stories and remembering better days. I also had work to see me through the next few months, the details of a legal case that I had brought against a former employer.

Those appointed rounds were perfect to assuage the early stages of grief, as nearly every day I was required to proofread documents, write up strategy papers, or sit through a deposition. Even the most basic lawsuit, like mine, can eat up hours and years, and most meetings end with uncertainty—about the opposition's strategies, the mood of the judge, or the quality of evidence. By comparison to a lawsuit, death is a clean break with the past, from which there are no appeals or motions for summary judgment.

In September I was back home in Europe. I wanted to be getting over the pain and thinking about the future, but little felt right. My mother's final days had lasted more than four years—with a broken hip, pneumonia, memory loss, and aspiration punctuating what might otherwise have been the gradual end of a life. I had been with her through this journey's end, as had my father and sisters, and that fall we all needed to step back from elderly cares and look to horizons that did not require Medicare forms, prescriptions, and what we called "weekend coverage."

To break with this past, I decided that I would make a trip around France by train and bicycle. What pushed me across the border that I see from my Swiss bedroom was not anything in particular connected with my mother's life. She might have loved Quimper china and the Impressionists, and she turned our childhood kitchen into what she called "the French café" (soft lighting, candles, and walls painted with fruit trees), but I did not associate my mother with France any more than with other European countries. She loved Provence and the Mediterranean shores but still spent most of her life in America.

I decided on France as the place to soften my sorrows because, despite living close to its border, there were many parts of the country I knew hardly at all. I had never been to *la France profonde* that stretches west of Lyon and south of Tours, nor did I know well Alsace or Lorraine or many of the wine regions. The places that I knew—Paris, Provence, and the Alps—were familiar from business trips or family vacations, but rarely had I been anywhere in France with my bicycle.

The plan was simple: I would buy a French rail pass, good for a number of days within two months' time. In between the train stations I would ride my bike, read my books, and stay in whatever hotels appeared on the horizon. I would pack my belongings in saddlebags—what the French call *panniers*—that had been kicking around the garage for thirty years, and I would take a Swiss army knife to make picnics more enjoyable and to pry open wine bottles.

While I was indifferent to my traveling comforts, I did have a precise idea of the places I wanted to see. I wanted to trace the arc of French history that connects the 1870–71 Franco-Prussian War, which started in Lorraine, to the disastrous peace treaty that was signed in 1919 at Versailles.

In between I would ride my bicycle to such places as Sedan, Verdun, Meuse-Argonne, Paris, Orléans, and Biarritz, where much of the drama between the Franco-Prussian War and the consequences of the peace treaty unfolded on battlefields or in regal drawing rooms. Along the way I would read from a pile of French histories that had, for years, been growing in the corner of my office. (Fortunately, I managed to condense many of them onto my Kindle.) They would narrate my travels, as I rode by train and bike on a wobbly diagonal from the northeast corner of France (Lorraine) to its southwest coast (Biarritz).

Only in Verdun and Paris would I would be revisiting places that I had gone to with my mother. On our first family trip to Europe, in spring 1970, my father rented a car on our last day and drove the five of us from Luxembourg to Verdun, to introduce us to the trenches that had outlined World War I. And on one of her last trips to Europe, to attend a family wedding, my mother and I spent a long weekend in Paris. For the rest I would be on roads that neither she or I had ever seen.

Practically speaking, I was traveling without GPS on my cell phone, so that at many crossroads I had to stop the bike and peer at the fine print of a Michelin road map. To complement my mapped route along many so-called D highways (those small white lines), I also brought with me battlefield maps that had I photocopied from histories. Often, as I ate breakfast in a hotel dining room, the manager or waiter would come by my table and laugh at all my maps, as though I were planning yet another invasion in Alsace or Lorraine. Nevertheless, I grew fond of plotting my course (on trains and small roads) across France, even if on occasion I would find myself riding into a dead end.

Sometimes I would find a local train station was out of service, and it would mean riding another ten kilometers to a larger rail junction. At other times, my small agricultural lane would turn into a mud track through the fields. But in all my travels across France, I never had a low moment. To be sure, I ate some makeshift meals and stayed in a few threadbare roadside hotels (many seemed to be named after Ferdinand Foch, the French general during World War I). But even sparse accommodation gave me pleasure, as I was doing things that I love by exploring the contours of history with books, a bike, and trains close by.

Because I was traveling in September and October, I generally had clear and crisp autumn weather, although occasionally I had to pedal through showers, and on several mornings in northeastern France, I woke up to find frost and fog thick on the ground. But usually I was riding in sunshine by eleven in the morning. Most evenings, before going to sleep, I would hand-wash my clothes from the day and dry them on a hotel radiator. That said, when I came home, I set out with a passion to assemble a wardrobe of drip-dry bicycle clothes, as there is nothing more discouraging than having to begin a day on the road with damp socks or pants.

The bicycle I rode across France—a Gary Fisher hybrid—was nothing special, but I valued it, as it also had a connection to my mother. During one of her many "final" illnesses (as I said, she hung on tenaciously for years and at one point shed even the deathly hallows of hospice), I took a break from her nursing rooms and stopped in a nearby bicycle store, as a distraction and to see what might be on sale. It was then February in New Jersey, when few riders are browsing for bikes. The store owner sized me up as someone in need of retail therapy, and he took three hundred dollars off the list price of the Gary Fisher. I still had to drag it home to Switzerland, so much of my savings went into excess baggage fees to the airline.

The bicycle came with disc brakes and thirty-two-millimeter tires, which were a godsend, especially on the cobblestones in cities such as Paris or Orléans. I cannot report that the Gary Fisher ate up the hills in, for example, the Meuse-Argonne, but it was sturdy companion throughout my travels, even when my saddlebags were laden with French history—if not the hovering presence of German chancellor Otto von Bismarck.

Many historians have made the connection between the French humiliations in the 1870–71 Franco-Prussian War and the harsh terms imposed on Germany at the end of World War I. But I had never read an account that describes some of the places of those wars and what they look like today. I had read books about visits to the trench battlefields in World War I and others about the breakdown in European diplomacy that led to four years of fighting over the lost province of Lorraine. But no book in my experience had described a visit to the principal battlefields of the Franco-Prussian War or tracked down where the likes of Clemenceau or Bismarck lived or worked. The abyss into which Europe fell between 1870 and 1919 is often depicted as some grand tableau of statesmen at court—all with their places numbered by the portrait artist—but I wanted to see what places such as Verdun and Gravelotte look like today, and then to imagine how the events there had shaped the modern world.

I also wanted to read extensively about the politics and battles that had so divided Europe. But to do that well, I needed to visualize the landscape that stretches between the German border and Biarritz, so that, for example, when I was reading about the 1870 German advance on Metz, I could see the hillside in my mind or imagine where it was that the French lines had broken. For me to read in depth about a subject or a place, I first need to see it, and then I don't remember what I have seen or read unless I write it down. It's why, when growing up, I should have attended something called the Bicycle and Train University of Diplomatic History and Politics, and written my term papers in cheap European two-star hotels. And that may be the college of letters that, since my formal graduation, I have ceaselessly tried to create—even if I am its only registered student.

I cannot tell you exactly why I decided to begin my travels in France with the battlefields of the Franco-Prussian War, but I can say that I knew almost nothing about them when I left home. I did know that the war had ended at Sedan; that was about it. Then at some point I recalled that, when I was growing up on Long Island, outside New York City, my aunt and uncle had moved from their large family house to a nearby apartment building. Their children were out of the house, and they were downsizing, which meant, as both of them worked in publishing, reducing the size of their substantial library.

Around the time that the movers were arriving, my mother drove me to her sister's house, which was, as might be expected, in chaos. But my aunt Hester found time to walk me to the bookshelves, where she encouraged me to take any book that I pleased. At the time I was about fifteen years old, and my aunt's and uncle's books seemed as imposing as the Library of Congress. In those days, I mostly read books about baseball and football, and my aunt and uncle didn't have much in their collection about Mickey Mantle or Joe Namath. Dutifully, I scanned the shelves and chose, as a keepsake, Michael Howard's *The Franco-Prussian War: The German Invasion of France 1870-1871*, which was first published in England. The type was microscopic, and the chapters of dense military history were devoted to such subjects as "The Army at Châlons" or "The Government of National Defense." I guess even at age fifteen I thought I ought to know more about French military history. But this particular book was beyond me.

As I went to college and afterward moved around, I kept the Howard book with me, perhaps thinking that someday I would be able to master the tactics of the Battle of Spicheren or understand where the French emperor threw down his sword. Only after my mother died, when I was hunting around my own library looking for ideas about where I might go on my bicycle in France, did I rediscover

Howard's 512-page tome, which in the intervening fifty years had not become much easier to read. (He writes in the dense style of an old-world military historian, with lots of divisional advances and corps flanking movements.) That said, if Howard's book is the reason that I headed on a bicycle toward Sedan after my mother's death, it deserves an honored place in my library. But I might shelve it in the section on grief therapy.

Flipping through some of the chapters, I finally saw where Sedan was in relation to Verdun (just up the road but across the American battlefields of the Meuse-Argonne), and where the Franco-Prussian War had ended in Orléans and Paris. These were all places that I could get to on the train with my rail pass and explore on my bicycle. And for whatever reason, they worked their magic on my soul. As I pieced together my rides, I went from being an aggrieved son, sad about the loss of my mother, to someone with his eyes fixed on the road ahead.

As I packed my saddlebags and set out for Lorraine, I knew it was more with my father (who was still living) that I shared conversations about the Franco-Prussian War, Napoleon III, Otto von Bismarck, Georges Clemenceau, and the Treaty of Versailles. (For example, he liked the aside of Queen Victoria's consort, Prince Albert, that Napoleon III "wishes for peace, enjoyment, and cheap corn.") But my mother had spent her professional life as a social worker concerned with others' mental and physical well-being, and I could easily imagine her nudging me on a dark day toward a bike ride in France, perhaps with the comforting words: "It would do you some good." Or as Honoré de Balzac wrote: "How Paris changes one's ideas!"

Biking with Bismarck

More Maginot Lines in Eastern France
Strasbourg

TO GET FROM GENEVA TO METZ—the besieged city of the Franco-Prussian war in northeastern France—I had to change trains in Basel and Strasbourg. In Basel, I only had time to buy a sandwich and walk the bike across the border (in the same building) to the French side of the railroad station. In Strasbourg, I had two hours to explore the European capital, where one week out of four the European Union relocates its deliberations from Brussels—at vast expense, with containers and moving trucks that shuttle everyone's inboxes and umbrella stands to the Alsatian frontier.

Strasbourg's shared capital status is the result of a French hissy fit at the time of European integration, so that France could claim that it was home to the European capital, here where Charlemagne a millennium earlier had his seat of power. On my only previous visit, all that I did with friends was walk around the city center, which a cathedral dominates, and peek into the many restaurants, galleries, and shops that fan out from the center on narrow cobblestoned streets and squares.

This time I had my bike, and I decided to ride along the river and see where the European Parliament has its headquarters. I found it several kilometers from the center, in ultramodern buildings that may explain, in small part, why the union is approaching dissolution. The parliament, surrounded by a number of equally modern administrative buildings, is housed in something that looks like *Star Trek*'s *Enterprise*.

The exterior is reflective glass, and the entire building looks like a starship, the prow of which faces toward the rest of Europe. (Later I wondered if maybe it wasn't a boomerang that had come back to haunt the French.) In an earlier generation, the Maginot Line ran through Strasbourg, its turrets also pointed toward the German frontier. The hope of the parliament is that its community regulations on such things as wine and butter production can achieve what André Maginot's line failed to do.

In glorious sunshine, I looped my bike around the parliament and navigated along river paths, until I was back at the Strasbourg railroad station, hunting for the train to Metz. Such an inconsequential local train was dwarfed amid the many high-speed TGVs (*train de grande vitesse*, meaning high speed) getting ready to race passengers to Paris, Lyon, Luxembourg, or Brussels. I found the coach marked with the silhouette of a bicycle, where I would hang my bike from hooks at the end of the car.

Never having biked in Lorraine, I spent the last twenty minutes of the train journey looking out the window at the hills around Metz, trying to figure out if the terrain was as up-and-down as I feared from my maps. The skyline of Metz appeared as an enchanted city—church spires disguised as the peaks of a king's crown—rising out of gently undulating valleys. I left the train, wondering how far I might get in the Indian-summer sunshine.

Not all French railroad stations are glorious, especially in second cities like Metz. This one had the look of a cathedral, one that had kept the faith of German militarism. Built between 1905 and 1908 with military appropriations from the German government—Metz was a spoil of the war in 1870—the station was designed with the goal of accommodating twenty-five thousand soldiers a day. Its completion allowed the German general staff to roll out the Schlieffen Plan that, at the start of World War I, concentrated troops in Lorraine and sent them on a long arc through northern France toward Paris. Metz was a designated hub for the German invasion forces, and the station, through which I walked with my bike on polished marble floors, felt as though it could at the same time both marshal and bless an invading army.

Another Napoleon Gets Whipped in Leipzig and Moscow

Metz

BECAUSE IT WAS A SUNDAY AFTERNOON, the medieval streets around Metz, especially those close to the soaring cathedral, were clogged with families pushing strollers and eating ice cream. Biking tenuously on the cobblestones, I felt relieved that the bike I had chosen for the trip had wider tires than the narrow ones used on racing bikes. During one of my mother's medical crises in Princeton, I had bought the bike on sale and dragged it home in a box. It was more of a hip urban machine than a touring bike, but I liked its disc brakes, aluminum frame, and sturdy rack, and was further pleased to find that the wheels were up to the task of riding on cobbled medieval streets.

Because I didn't want to leave my saddlebags unattended on the sidewalk, I only rode around the outside of the cathedral. Nevertheless, I loved the feel of Metz, with small restaurants perched over canals and elegant streets filled with small cafés. Much of the city walls remain, and I enjoyed biking through the old gates, imagining Metz as the bulwark of French civilization for almost two thousand years.

During the Franco-Prussian War, the army of French marshal François Achille Bazaine was besieged in Metz and eventually surrendered, to the disgrace of the French nation. Among the incompetencies of the French commander was his failure to find a large store of ammunition kept at the Metz railroad station, something he bequeathed to the invading Germans when he ran up the white flag in October 1870.

As in Strasbourg, I was tempted in Metz to tuck into a Sunday lunch and call it a day over Alsatian wine and afternoon coffee. But I had more than three hours of daylight left, and I was eager to ride my bike to the Franco-Prussian battlefields that lie to the west of the city, in the hills that crown the area. In places such as Gravelotte, Mars-la-Tour, and Vionville, Bazaine had failed to defeat the German army. That forced him to retreat to Metz, where his war and that of his army would end.

Instead of a proper Sunday meal, I washed down a cheese sandwich with a cold beer, bolted strong coffee, nibbled chocolate, filled up my water bottles in the small café, and set my bike for Gravelotte, which on the map was just west of the city. Leaving Metz, however, I fared little better than Bazaine. Once through a portcullis, I ended up in the dead end of the University of Lorraine, a dreary modern campus of functional buildings built around a cul-de-sac.

Retracing my tracks, I found the right road out of town. Gravelotte turned out to be at the top of a long hill that took almost an hour to ascend, with my shortening breaths a distant echo of the trucks that passed me, also groaning in their lowest gears. At least I was climbing toward hamlets that had the evocative names of Moscow and Leipzig. From time to time I stopped to drink water and look around at hills that had the look of a petrified ocean, in which the crests were boulders, soft meadows, or sharp defiles.

In the initial retreat from the German frontier in August 1870, the French emperor, Napoleon III, had taken his troops along the same route I was now riding, although he was fleeing into a fatal trap, as the Germans had another army between Metz and Verdun to the west. In an account of this retreat, the historian Geoffrey Wawro writes in *The Franco-Prussian War: The German Conquest of France in 1870-1871*:

> As the emperor crested the Amanvillers ridge behind Metz – a broad shoulder of hills that would shortly be the scene of the war's decisive battle – he asked the names of the two picturesque hamlets on the road down to Gravelotte. Local legend had it that he sat and brooded when told the answer: "Moscow and Leipzig." He ought to have brooded: The French military defeats at Moscow in 1812 and Leipzig in 1813 had unraveled his illustrious uncle's First Empire; Gravelotte would unravel his.

Gravelotte in 1870
"Worse than a crime; it was a blunder"

RIDING TOWARD GRAVELOTTE into the setting sun, I got into a rhythm, spinning my lowest gears and thinking about how Napoleon III and his commanding general Bazaine managed to position his army so incompetently that the Germans were attacking from the west and the French had their backs to Metz. These thoughts might have been high-minded for a bike trip, but it kept me from getting discouraged on the switchbacks.

War was declared in summer 1870, ostensibly over the insults contained in the now-famous Ems Dispatch, a cable that the French sent to the German kaiser, Wilhelm I, while he was taking the waters at Ems, a royal retreat of spas and other thermal cures. The French were upset that the kaiser had violated an understanding about the appointment of the next king of Spain. (The German leader had nominated one of his princelings.)

The dispatch voiced the usual diplomatic objections and would not have led to an outbreak of war, except that Prussian Chancellor Otto von Bismarck, back in Berlin and looking for a military opportunity that would allow Prussia to square its accounts with France, released to the press a redacted version of the Ems Dispatch, which made it seem as though the French had insulted the kaiser.

When that incident prompted war fevers in Germany, Napoleon III decided he had no choice—especially given his martial lineage—but to mobilize his armies and invade Germany in the area around Saarbrücken. Although he was initially successful, in a matter of days the mobilized German forces counterattacked and pushed the French back across the border. The German army won several stunning victories at Wissembourg and Wörth, enabling it in August 1870 to divide its forces and encircle Metz, and much of Napoleon III's army. One French force, led by Marshal Patrice MacMahon, escaped to the west of the encircling Germans, while Bazaine's men were trapped between the blocking Germans and the fortress city of Metz. As Talleyrand said earlier in French history: "It was worse than a crime; it was a blunder."

The hill on which the twisting road crested looked down into the Gravelotte ravine, although nothing marked it as the high ground in such a titanic battle. Instead, small posted warning signs indicated that the fields on either side of the road were part of a military reservation and contained unexploded ordnance. Was it possible that shells from the battle in August 1870 were still a threat to hikers and mountain bike riders?

Weaving on my bike, I could look back toward the spires of Metz and forward into a valley that I knew had once been a vale of tears. Into this ravine and up the slope on which I was standing, the Germans had sent waves of infantry into entrenched French lines, which were well armed with a celebrated rifle, the Chassepot, that was more accurate at a longer range than any similar gun in the German army. The rifle might have made the difference in this and other battles of the war, except that the German army had superior accuracy and firepower with their artillery, and whenever a battle hung in the balance, it was soon decided with heavy shells.

Instead of freewheeling down the long incline into the valley and then pedaling up the other side into Gravelotte, I went slowly down the hill, stopping here and there on the busy road to look at markers in the underbrush that denoted the forward advance of various German companies and squads. Sometimes the spot was marked with a white cross. In other places, a larger obelisk was enclosed with an iron fence. All the now-forgotten monuments that I saw by walking into the overgrown fields were German, and all the markers were faded from neglect. Clearly the attacking German forces had been given suicidal orders—to fight uphill against an enemy with clear fields of fire from all angles. Only later would they discover the truth of author Philip Guedalla's conclusion: "Like its generals, the army of the Second Empire was brave, uneducated, and adapted to the special purposes of colonial warfare."

Gravelotte is a nondescript farming village at the top of the ravine, where the two armies collided in a battle of Gettysburg proportions. It was equally indecisive—except that Bazaine withdrew into the city of Metz, which was besieged, and two months later he surrendered 150,000 troops.

One eyewitness to the battle was the American general Philip Sheridan, who was sent by President Ulysses S. Grant to observe the war from the German side. Sheridan had fought in many battles of the American Civil War. Most memorably, in 1864 he cleared the Shenandoah Valley of Confederate cavalry. Later he was ruthless in waging war on the Great Plains against Native American tribes, and to him is attributed the quote "The only good Indian is a dead Indian," although what he may have said is "The only good Indians I ever saw were dead." He is also the one who said that if he "owned Texas and Hell, I would rent Texas and live in Hell." Sheridan liked the Prussian officers and men with whom he rode ("very good brave fellows") but reported to Grant that "there is nothing to be learned here professionally."

As an observer at Gravelotte, Sheridan wrote that "the ground over which an approach to the French line had to be made was essentially a natural open glacis, that could be thoroughly swept by the fire of the defenders." The quotation appears in Wawro's *The Franco-Prussian War: The German Conquest of France 1870-1871*, one of only two accounts in print of the conflict in English, the other being Michael Howard's *The Franco-Prussian War: The German Invasion of France in 1870-1871*.

Before setting out on my ride, I had downloaded Wawro's book to my Kindle, and I had read much of it before coming to this valley of decision. Wawro has vivid descriptions of the kaiser and the senior officers who were leading the attack against the French lines. He writes:

Just beyond Gravelotte, this perturbed royal headquarters had a famous encounter with [General Karl Friedrich von] Steinmetz. "Why are the men not advancing?" the king demanded. "They have no more leaders; their officers are all dead or wounded," Steinmetz replied. Jostled by fleeing soldiers, the king grabbed at the passing troops and demanded that they return to their units. "They are cowards," he muttered to no one in particular. This enraged [Field Marshal Helmuth von] Moltke, who burst out: "But the men are dying like heroes for Your Majesty!" The king gave his staff chief an icy look and spat out, "I alone will be the judge of that." Moltke turned and angrily rode away, leaving his royal majesty alone near the Mance ravine.

Given that more than thirty thousand men on both sides were casualties at Gravelotte, I was surprised that the town, up another long hill, had so little to commemorate the battle. The guidebook mentioned a museum, although I rode all over the small town and saw no sign of it.

Marshal Bazaine Plays a Bad Game
of Backgammon
Vionville

THE ONLY MEMORIAL OF ANY KIND that I found in Gravelotte was a small cemetery off the main road, in which the graves on the left side are German and on the right French. I found the expressions of sacrifice more poignant on the German headstones than those of the French. Perhaps the French chose to forget Gravelotte because Bazaine's bizarre style of command turned it from a French victory into a German victory?

Commissioned from the ranks in 1833 and a veteran of many colonial engagements, Bazaine had served with bravery and distinction in North Africa and Crimea before a tour of duty in Mexico during the farce that Napoleon III staged, which had an Austrian archduke, Maximilian, sitting on the Mexican throne. Bazaine's uncle Napoleon I had sold Louisiana to the Americans; now the equally ambitious nephew, who was long on pomp whatever the circumstance, sought a return engagement to the New World in Mexico.

Under the terms of the Monroe Doctrine, the Americans should have closed the light opera after a few runs in Mexico City, except that when it opened in 1864 the American South had seceded from the Union and President Abraham Lincoln had not the troops to spare to remove the French from the Western Hemisphere. During the Civil War the best Lincoln could do—and it was a considerable achievement—was to keep both Napoleon III and the English government from recognizing the Confederacy. Without that link, Maximilian withered on his supply lines.

Meanwhile, Bazaine fought with distinction against the rebel Mexican forces of Benito Juárez until the American Civil War ended and U.S. troops were sent to make threatening moves along the Mexican border. By now a marshal, Bazaine was withdrawn, and returned to a hero's welcome in France, while the less fortunate Maximilian was eased off his Mexican throne with a firing squad.

After the opening scenes of the Franco-Prussian War went so poorly for the French along the German border, Napoleon III appointed Bazaine his supreme commander, as the emperor's army was divided (with the Germans in between), and his nerves were not up to the demands of modern warfare. One of Bazaine's biographers, Philip Guedalla, writes in *The Two Marshals*: "It may be doubted if Napoleon himself could have played the cards dealt by Napoleon III to Bazaine." Nevertheless, Bazaine was outflanked repeatedly on the road to Gravelotte, losing battles at places such as Vionville, Rezonville, and Mars-la-Tour before the Germans started sending their regiments up the hill in the Mance ravine.

In the command of his divisions at Gravelotte, Bazaine had little feel for the ebb and flow of the battle. Nor did he communicate with his subordinates. As one said (as is quoted in Wawro): "I spent the entire day in complete ignorance of

Marshal Bazaine's intentions, or of any ultimate objective." One report has him, during the height of the battle, playing backgammon in a shelter.

Bazaine had no answer for German artillery, which punched large holes in the French defenses. Wawro writes: "Despite superior positions – most German accounts spoke of seeing nothing but French kepis [caps] throughout the battle – the French lost thousands of dead, wounded, and missing to the Prussian cannon." Bazaine's men fought as well at Gravelotte as did General George Meade's at Gettysburg, yet each man's reputation would founder in their lack of pursuit at battle's end. Meade refused to attack Robert E. Lee as the Confederates withdrew south from Gettysburg, and Bazaine retreated from the heights overlooking Gravelotte into Metz. Wawro quotes one astounded French soldier: "Now, tonight, after a victorious battle . . . when the road to Verdun had been secured with the blood of 20,000 men, we retreated! Toward Metz!"

What accounts for such a defeatist decision? Guedalla quotes Bazaine as saying: "After all, we must save the army, and for that we must go back to Metz." The fortress city might have offered the French army refuge and proved a tough nut for the Germans to crack, except that Metz had insufficient food and (known) ammunition for it to be anything other than a death trap. Proving to be fatal to the French army, Bazaine made little effort, when faced with the reality of his supply situation, to fight his way out of Metz, either to save his army or link up with the army of Marshal MacMahon, then curiously marching north toward his own destiny at Sedan.

Under siege, Bazaine was strangely passive, as though on a routine assignment and waiting for another officer to relieve him. Slowly the Germans tightened the noose around Metz, taking the surrounding hills and forts and keeping the French from resupplying the garrison. Later Bazaine would be tried and convicted of treason over his surrender of the French army in Metz. In his own defense, he said: "I did not feel that I had the right to make a vain sacrifice for empty glory of those lives that were so precious to their country and their families." The court-martial believed none of it, and he was imprisoned on a rock in the Mediterranean until, like the Count of Monte Cristo, he made a daring escape and lived the rest of his life on the run and in exile.

Sacred Ways to Verdun
Mars-la-Tour

WITHOUT FINDING THE GRAVELOTTE MUSEUM, I rode west across the battlefields that had led to Gravelotte: Rezonville, Vionville, and Mars-la-Tour. At one time their names might have resonated with French and German soldiers as later armies would remember Normandy, Bastogne, or Khe Sanh. Now, however, the Franco-Prussian War has lost most of its followers.

Along the route I saw markers for this unit or that fallen officer, but often moss covered the inscriptions, and the villages go about their farming business without much concern for those who gave their last full measure of devotion in fields now expansive with wheat.

Another reason why the Germans prevailed in this expansive landscape is that they were willing to charge emplaced guns and trenches with their horses. The results were horrific for the chargers, but their daring unnerved Bazaine, who sensed an enemy more mobile and widespread than they were. Ironically, these were the last rolls of the dice for the Germans. The elderly General Karl Friedrich von Steinmetz knew he was down to his last reserves but was willing to try anything to sustain the attack. His formations might have crumbled had Bazaine chosen to counterattack.

The French, however, believed only the worst from each cavalry encounter and slowly fell back on Gravelotte and Metz. Of one such exchange, Wawro writes:

> "Von Bredow's Death Ride" was a rare instance of a successful cavalry charge against modern rifles and artillery. Though Bredow lost 420 of his 800 men – one of whom was Bismarck's son Herbert, who fell wounded – he overran Canrobert's corps artillery, panicked his trains, and caused Bazaine to sink even deeper into his defensive redoubt around Gravelotte.

I stopped in most villages, taking pictures of monuments and road signs—including several for the Voie Sacrée (Sacred Way), commemorating the 1944 route that the army of U.S. general George Patton took to Germany after the D-Day landings in Normandy. (A more celebrated Voie Sacrée connected Verdun in World War I to its supply depots in Bar-le-Duc, forty miles west of the trenches.)

Except for the setting sun in my eyes, the late summer afternoon was ideal for biking. I had a slight breeze at my back, leading me to think for a while that I might make it all the way to Verdun before it got too dark. Instead, around 7 p.m. I turned north at Mars-la-Tour and headed toward the station of Jarny, where I knew there was a local train to Verdun.

Both Mars-la-Tour and Jarny struck me as sad. In rural France toward sunset, especially in Lorraine, it felt as though most of the population was still hiding from invading armies. The sidewalks were empty, and the drab storefronts shuttered, awaiting either morning or renewed economic prosperity. In the United States, out-of-town malls have drained the lifeblood out of similar towns.

In France, the decline is the result of migration to Paris and the industrial centers, and the fact that agricultural corporations can run their farms largely with machines. The only bright lights I saw came from tattoo parlors or shops selling beer and betting. By following signs marked "SNCF" (the national railway, officially called *la Société nationale des chemins de fer français*), I found the station and, just as pleasing, a Verdun train due in twenty minutes.

I passed the time reading a memorial marker outside the station, describing the fate (shot, deported, imprisoned, interned, tortured) of World War II resistance members and local Jews from Jarny. Names like Buchenwald, Mauthausen, Bergen-Belsen, and Sachsenhausen followed brief descriptions of the time and place when the victims were arrested or taken prisoner. A hand-drawn map had *X*s to mark the villages where many had lived, and the surrounding photos had more defiant remembrances, with pictures of German trains blown up at the station or derailed down the line.

My own train arrived a few minutes late, on its forty-mile run from Metz to Verdun. I stood with my bike rather than hanging it from a hook in the car. About twenty minutes later I was in Verdun and searching for a hotel where I could lodge with my bike. A book about bike touring had counseled me before leaving that locks, just adding weight, were unnecessary on a tour. I had followed the advice, choosing instead to burden my saddlebags with a laptop computer and maps. It meant that in picking a hotel, I always needed to find a safe place to leave my bike, and that could take time.

Verdun after dark was as quiet as a tomb, befitting its tragic past. Nevertheless, its streets and facades were lit, giving it an elegance that I found comforting after the emptiness

When I left the Hotel Verdun that morning, heading up toward Le Champ de Bataille, I had among my papers Fussell's Maurice Muel pamphlet titled "Verdun, the Noble Fortress." Because it dates to the late 1970s, the pictures inside are black and white, and the cars parked near some of the historic monuments look as though the Pink Panther could have driven them.

The Folly of Nationalism
"If you haven't seen Verdun,
you haven't seen anything of the war."

THE VERDUN TRENCHES, CEMETERIES, forts, and preserved lands lie to the northeast of the town, on what are called the Meuse heights—the Meuse being the north-south river that formed one of the natural borders between French and German lines in World War I, even though it is more a stream than a great European river.

In striking out from Verdun that morning, I wanted to enter the battlefield forests from the south. First I had to ascend a long hill that made it clear that the battle—at its worst from February to November 1916—was for the high ground around Verdun. Although German artillery reduced the town of Verdun to rubble, the town was never occupied, and the worst fighting took place in a long arc around its perimeter.

At least the weather was in my favor, cool with clear skies. Still in town, I passed a national cemetery and then pedaled for half an hour up a long hill to a sign marked "Champ de Bataille 14-18 (Battlefield 1914-18)." On it were indicated the two forts, Vaux and Douaumont, around which so many of the casualties in the fighting were sustained. In all, it is estimated that the French had 378,777 men killed, wounded, or missing in the battle, while casualties for the Germans were 330,000. Survivors would say: "If you haven't seen Verdun, you haven't seen anything of the war."

From the busy main road with fast cars and lumbering trucks, I entered the thick Verdun forest, broken only by a park service road and occasional markers that explained the disposition of the forces during the long battle. At one signpost I leaned my bike against a tree and walked into the forest as directed by a map—to climb a wooden set of stairs that overlook the remains of a trench line. The war was fought a hundred years ago, but here and there the vestiges of trenches and dugouts remain, filled now with fallen leaves and trees, limbs of a different kind than those blown about in 1916.

One senses the passage of time when looking at the Verdun front lines among the trees, as during fighting they would have looked like the dark side of the moon, with craters and no vegetation. One account describes the barren landscape: "The sheer number of the shells and the systematic rhythm in which they fell—saturating one stretch of ground before moving on to the next—made it look, some said, as if the forests were being doused by a hosepipe that destroyed everything it touched."

I found Fort de Vaux on a dead-end road. The gift shop had yet to open, so I leaned my bike against the ramparts that are dug into the hillside and walked on top of the fort, which for the most part is carved into a bluff that overlooks the plains stretching toward Metz. On top of the fort are benches and grass, as if it were a city park with gun emplacements. (Appropriately, one of the plaques celebrates the war contributions of carrier pigeons.) In this case, the word "fort" does not mean a medieval garrison but a redoubt that was to guard the heights from a German "push."

The Germans chose Verdun for their attacks in 1916, in part, because of the tactics that had worked so well at Gravelotte in 1870. They wanted the French to concentrate their armies in an enclosed area so they could destroy them piecemeal with artillery in a battle of attrition. In turn, the French chose to make a stand on the Meuse Heights because they had invested the landscape with what Fussell calls "national virtue and survival," not to mention "myth, ritual, and romance."

In *The Road to Verdun: World War I's Most Momentous Battle and the Folly of Nationalism*, which I read only after my bike rides, the excellent historian Ian Ousby makes points similar to Fussell's. He believes that places such as Fort de Vaux, facing the plains toward Gravelotte and Metz, embodied all the complex feelings that lingered after the defeats in 1870. He writes:

> In my prologue I argued that ground always has an emotional content in battle, usually invested in it by what has happened before. The commemoration of sites such as Mars-la-Tour by the French and Gravelotte by the Germans had begun to give ground exactly the sort of emotional content that would help shape the particular course of the First World War. . . .
>
> A few kilometers beyond Gravelotte and the new border lay Mars-la-Tour, where the French had put their monument and were busy holding their ceremonies, and not far beyond Mars-la-Tour lay Verdun. So the road between the two cities linked a cluster, not just of battlefield sites

but of commemorated sites: what French rhetoric had come to call *lieux sacrés*, "holy places" or "sacred soil."

The purpose of Fort de Vaux was to guard that *voie sacrée* from the heights.

When the gift shop and small museum opened, I browsed through the books for sale, buying a copy of *Le Feu* (*Under Fire*) by Henri Barbusse, a French novel of the trenches. ("We've seen too much to remember.") I bought some postcards, especially for my father, who in 1970, on our first family trip to Europe, rented a car in Luxembourg to take us to Verdun. At that point I knew nothing about it. (My school history classes had a habit of running out of time before either the first or second world wars were covered.) In 1970 the family had been on the Grand Tour, although instead of London, Paris, and Berlin, my father had taken us to Austria, Italy, and Yugoslavia, places his own mother had taken him when he was a baby in 1920.

Awaiting the propeller Icelandic Airlines flight home to New York from Luxembourg, he decided there was time to spend a day at Verdun. He rented a car, and we set off after breakfast, on what was an hour's drive in memory, although what is most vivid is that we saw a motorcycle accident on the way. Without the least hesitation, my father had stopped the car and gone to the aid of the bloodied rider—one of the few times in my life I saw firsthand his natural instincts as an infantry officer.

Like Fussell, my father came out of college to lead men into World War II battles, although his were on Pacific islands, not in the European theater. Unlike Fussell, who was wounded shortly after he went up to the front lines, my father survived more than three years of combat at places such as

Guadalcanal, Cape Gloucester, and Peleliu. For whatever reason—was it Marine Corps cynicism about army training?—my father never warmed to Fussell's books, especially *Wartime*, which he found "overwritten and exaggerated." He would say he never felt himself to be "expendable." He did not leave his company "dead or wounded," although many did. Nor did he find distant kinship with the delicate English sentiments of the war poets. I never knew him to read Sassoon or Rupert Brooke. He preferred the steely determination of French officers, those who later said about Verdun: "I was there" or "I did Verdun" (*"J'ai fait Verdun"*).

Growing up, I remember many books on my father's shelves with titles like *Education Before Verdun*, no doubt the reason he did not want to miss seeing the battlefield when we were so close by in Luxembourg. After the drama of the motorcycle accident, we drove to a vast French cemetery, the dominating ossuary with the bones of unknown soldiers and, most memorable to me, a trench that had bayonets sticking out of the sand, as though a bombshell had buried the men alive even as they were ready go over the top against the Germans.

The imagery of the trench stayed with me, even after I read that the memorial, in all likelihood, was a fabrication of postwar grief and political haymaking (against the Germans) by Georges Clemenceau, among others. According to Jay Winter's *Sites of Memory, Sites of Mourning: The Great War in European Cultural History*, "the Trench of the Bayonets, like the Battle of Verdun itself, became the stuff of myth . . . [even] during the war." Instead of the German shell burying the men at the ready, with only the tips of their bayonets protruding from the dirt, he writes, "common sense suggests that they were buried by bombardment, and that their graves were marked by the German soldiers who, briefly, had occupied this sector."

An American banker visiting Verdun after the war came upon the mass grave and offered to Clemenceau to build a Romanesque tomb above the trench, giving the monument the additional bonds of French-American solidarity. Winter writes that, unusually, the "Trench of the Bayonets is a war memorial of a special kind: a tomb frozen in time and preserved not *by*, but *from* art." By contrast, much of Verdun is remembered with heroic monuments, dominated at the center by the ossuary that is surrounded by the vineyard of white crosses that seem to stretch across the horizon.

Charles de Gaulle Waves the White Flag
Douaumont

FROM FORT DE VAUX, I stopped at the Verdun War Memorial museum, which is complete with cannons, barbed wire, uniforms, and trenches, although there again I spent most of my time in the bookshop. I discovered Ousby's history, which caught my eye as I, too, felt I was on the road to Verdun. He writes in a style that is more accessible than, say, Fussell's, who in *The Great War and Modern Memory* can retreat into the language of his postwar profession, academic English criticism. For example, he writes: "Since war takes place outdoors, and always within nature, its symbolic status is that of the ultimate anti-pastoral."

Ousby's point about Verdun is that by its location near the battlefield humiliations of 1870, France felt it had little choice but to leave its army in the cauldron of German attacks and artillery, no matter how many casualties were suffered. That led to orders that varied little from death sentences—for men to hold their ground and trenches no matter what.

Ousby quotes several times the orders dispatched to a brave officer who wanted to withdraw his men to safety behind a line of bombardments. Nevertheless, the commanding officer responded, "My poor Robin, your orders are to stay here." All orders at Verdun were a variation on the same theme, and often ended with men buried in their trenches.

Just beyond the national cemetery is a small road that leads to Fort de Douaumont, which Ousby describes as the core of many myths that grew up around Verdun, both during the war and after.

Similar in construction to Vaux, the fort is dug into a hillside, and the outer shell, now covered with grass, bristles with gun pits. I found a place to leave my unlocked bike and walked as I had at Vaux, remembering the 1970 visit here with my father and how, during random conversations about World War I afterward, he would sigh with relief that he never had to command men in trenches. By comparison, I am sure later French Legionnaires were glad they never had to fight for months on end in the Guadalcanal jungle.

The Germans captured Douaumont, which redoubled the determination of the French to hold the line at Verdun and recapture something sacred that had been lost in the national psyche. Ousby writes: "The loss of Douaumont had changed the temper of the entire battle, had cemented a determination that was no longer just local but now a national commitment." Sadly, the only tactics employed at Verdun were to hang on, summed up in the French phrase *"Il faut tenir,"* which means: "We must hold."

Ousby describes how dying in the lines "became a national obsession." That led, in turn, to tactics that equated slaughter with the proof that the French would not let go. Although to the men suffering and dying in the lines such patriotic sentiments made no sense (Robert Graves observed that they were "fit only for civilians, or prisoners"), the French nation romanticized the battle as all that was worth defending in the war. Ousby writes: "Above all, Douaumont was as a woman: a beautiful French woman, another daughter of France abused and defiled."

Under no such illusions, the men up front called Verdun "the hungry octopus" or "the slaughterhouse," and named roads Chemin de l'abattoir (Slaughterhouse Way), as they led only to death. At the beginning of the war, they had been sent to the front only with the idea of attacking with the bayonet. (That was French tactical thinking for much of the battle and the war.) When that didn't work ("*Élan*, so dear to the French soul, and all other warrior virtues no longer decided anything"), all anyone could do, including "my poor Robin," was stand their ground. Ousby writes: "If Verdun was a storm at sea, the French troops were not just shipwrecked mariners on their raft but something more pitiable: Robinson Crusoes in their ragged and unkempt appearance, and also in the terrible fact of abandonment."

If there was a national hero at Verdun, it was Marshal Philippe Pétain, to whom the expression "They shall not pass" is attributed, although in all likelihood he borrowed it from men in the lines or from General Robert Nivelle (of whom the men in the ranks said, "He appeared as stiff as if he had swallowed a sword"). Although Pétain would later become a national disgrace for his Nazi collaborations as the leader of Vichy France, at Verdun he is credited with having organized the Voie Sacrée to keep supplies flowing to the front.

Pétain's military genius, if he had any, was that he was by instinct defensive, in a war that was largely led by generals ordering Napoleonic charges over the top. His temperament suited the landscape around Verdun, in that he didn't mind suffering casualties while holding on, which in this case fed his defensive outlook and the national obsession to hold the line. A critic, Marc Boasson, said: "This is not heroism. It's ignominy." Nevertheless, though in 1917 and 1918 he was passed over for supreme command for lacking any ideas about how the war might be ended—making him little different from the men in the lines who said, "I did Verdun"— Pétain emerged from the battle as the national savior,

After World War II, General Charles de Gaulle was in power when Pétain was sentenced to death (later commuted) for his Vichy collaborations. At Verdun, de Gaulle had been a junior officer, serving in Pétain's old 33rd Regiment and sharing a close relationship with his former regimental officer. During the battle, as Ousby and others have recounted, de Gaulle was taken prisoner after his position near Fort Douaumont was shelled and overrun with German troops.

The historical question, to which there are few concrete answers, is whether de Gaulle surrendered too readily to the Germans. (If so, he would not have been the only one in the French army who, to save his life, did what the men in the lines called *faire Kamerad*—surrender by shouting out the German word for "comrade.") In the dispatches of the battle, Pétain and other senior officers praised de Gaulle for his courage while leading his men in battle (Ousby writes: "Replete with all the heroic imagery of a nineteenth century canvas, the account spoke of shattered rifles and exhausted ammunition, of hand-to-hand struggle with the closely packed ranks of the enemy."), although a German veteran of the battle asserted that "de Gaulle and his men had surrendered under a white flag improvised from a shirt on the end a rifle."

De Gaulle himself never provided a detailed account of what happened when he was captured in the woods. No doubt, after World War II, when Pétain saw de Gaulle do nothing to commute his death sentence, he must have wondered why he had been so eager to recommend the ambitious colonel for the Légion d'honneur at Verdun. Perhaps Pétain wasn't the only one with experience of *faire Kamerad?*

Le Mort Homme in the Shadows
Chattancourt

FROM THE TRENCH OF THE BAYONETS, I descended toward
the Meuse in sweeping turns and through forests that continue to guard their secrets. To get to the northwest sector
of the Verdun battle lines, I crossed the river at Charny and
began a climb that stayed with me for the next several hours,
although in only a few places did it force me to stand on my
pedals or weave across the road. Between Charny and Chattancourt the road crossed gentle open farmland and had little
car traffic, compared with the pilgrims driving slowly around
the contours of tourist Verdun.

At Chattancourt, I saw signs for Le Mort Homme (the
Dead Man), a bitterly contested hill during the war, but wondered whether I needed to ride up such a sharp incline. The
road looked like a ski slope cut out of the trees. While cir-
cling around the farm houses in Chattancourt, I weighed
obeisance to historical due diligence against a twenty-minute
climb in midday heat.

In the village, a moss-covered plaque noted that Chattancourt had 316 inhabitants in 1901, 233 in 1961, and 165 in
1996. Clearly, having a world war fought around it did not
help the population between 1914 and 1918, while the recent
declines spoke volumes about the evolution of rural France.

Although it was a bright sunny September day, I saw no one in the village center, as though they were all away on a school trip or perhaps watching the World Cup.

Diligence won out over my tired legs, and I rode up Le Mort Homme, struggling for the last hundred meters and then sitting on a bench to drink water from my bottles. The monument in the clearing cut from the forest shows a man, perhaps a skeleton, wrapped in cloth and holding a scepter. Were he reclining, he might be about to enter his grave, but he is standing, defiantly, above the words *"Ils n'ont pas passé"* ("They did not pass"). The scepter and the flowing robes symbolize the strength not just of ordinary soldiers but of France, and there was a time when Le Mort Homme resonated with the last stands of places such as Bastogne or Singapore. Now, however, it is forgotten.

Riding up and down the hill, I saw no one in the area. Not even the symbolism of the hill draws the crowds. For a long time Le Mort Homme was remembered because a French counterattack, with bayonets, had kept the Germans from overrunning the hill, from which they could have fired artillery or swept down on Verdun, seven miles to the south across open land. An account of that bayonet attack reads: "With *élan* carrying us forward, we reached the crest."

Ousby, however, puts it in context:

The years spent in the abyss after 1870-71 had brought self-critical comment on the gulf separating *élan* from the steady, methodical application that the French took to be the core of the German mentality. Yet in *élan* also lay, eventually, the recovery from humiliation.

He concludes: "To Verdun men had brought complex and bitter memories of 1870–71; from Verdun they took memories yet more complex and bitter, to fuel the next stage in the cycle of national confrontation."

From Le Mort Homme, riding up an incline to Esnes-en-Argonne, I began to search for lunch and more water. The midday sun was hot, and I had emptied my bottles and eaten the food I had carried away from breakfast at the hotel. Usually in France roadside cafés are plentiful, and I could never remember in other travels being far from food and drink. Today was different.

The towns I passed through were without stores or restaurants. The center squares had small war memorials, maybe a flag, and that was it. Knowing that I was heading up yet another long hill, past Côte 304—another contested bluff in the Mort Homme sector—I was reduced to collecting apples that had fallen from roadside trees. For water, I helped myself from a farmer's spigot.

Fortified with this makeshift snack, I had the energy to get over the last hill and down to the village of Malancourt, which was not only contested in 1916 but also acted as a staging area for American troops when, in September 1918, they jumped off into the biggest American battle of World War I, known as Meuse-Argonne.

Although I did not stay long in Malancourt—I took pictures, ate another fallen apple, and drank water—I found the village as evocative of the Great War as any I would pass. The war memorial on the main road was shaped from a boulder and faced simply with helmets, shell casings, and a white cross. I read a plaque about the father of a missing soldier who took it upon himself to get to Malancourt and search for his son—an impulse that every parent of the missing in the war must have shared, but that few were able to carry out. His grief in that narrow ravine that cuts through the village must have been like that of King Priam, begging Achilles to return his slain son, Hector. Robert Fagles writes in his translation of the *Iliad*:

> But one, one was left me, to guard my walls, my people—
> the one you killed the other day, defending his fatherland,
> my Hector! It's all for him that I have come to the ships now,
> to win him back from you—I bring a priceless ransom.
> Revere the gods, Achilles! Pity me in my own right,
> remember your own father! I deserve more pity.

Black Jack Pershing Deals Bad Cards
Meuse-Argonne

STARTING UP THE HILL OUT OF MALANCOURT, I was no longer in Verdun, but in the landscape of the Meuse-Argonne
campaign that, in less than three months, was to cost the
United States more lives than were lost in twenty years of the
Vietnam War. Before leaving on this trip with my bike, I had
only a vague sense where the Argonne was. I knew it was in
France, obviously, but I thought it was closer to the Marne
and Belleau Wood, early American encounters in the war. It
was at Belleau Wood that Marine Corps Gunnery Sergeant
Dan Daly is said to have exhorted his men: "Come on, you
sons of bitches. Do you want to live forever?"[1]

Only when I began poring over my maps on the train
ride to Metz did I figure out that the Argonne Forest lay
between Verdun and Sedan and that it would make a perfect
bike ride between the two cities. Nor did I know, before I set
off from Malancourt, that the fighting in the Argonne was an
American tragedy on the scale of what later would be seen in
Vietnam. From my previous reading, I had somehow thought
that the campaign had helped to tilt World War I in favor of

1: My father had the quote on one of his USMC coffee mugs and would often say
to his caregiver, Alex Atiemo: "I can't believe a Marine would say that to his men."

the Allies and that American determination had broken the stalemate along the trenches. Now, however, I understand it as a near-useless slaughter that only pushed American politics deeper into the quicksands of militarism.

From Malancourt I had a five-kilometer ride uphill to Montfaucon, where there is a large American memorial that dominates the skyline of a small hilltop town. In the Argonne campaign that began on September 2, 1918, that hillside was among the early objectives, one that came at a far higher price than General John J. "Black Jack" Pershing had imagined at his planning boards. The Americans' goal in the campaign was to fight north to seize Sedan and the rail line to Mézières, which they did, but only at the cost of nearly destroying their army.

Pershing hoped his troops might get to Sedan in a week or so, as the distance is less than fifty miles. (By bike, less than a day.) As it turned out, the war would end before the Americans got to Sedan, and the offensive would consume 117,000 casualties (of which twenty-six thousand were killed) and deploy more than one million soldiers. It may have been an excellent military school for future commanders—among those who fought in the campaign were George Marshall, George Patton, Harry Truman, and Douglas MacArthur— but it was also a showcase of military incompetence.

Pershing's First Army assembled for the Argonne offensive after closing the Saint-Mihiel salient, which is southeast of Verdun. I had seen signs for Saint-Mihiel when riding out of Gravelotte but decided against such a detour. In that engagement, the American army eliminated a bulge in the German lines and then shifted its forces around Verdun to a line that stretched east to west from the river Meuse to the

Argonne Forest, which I could see in the distance on my left as I rode toward Montfaucon. It showed itself as clumps of trees on small, squat hills.

In *To Conquer Hell: The Meuse-Argonne, 1918*, the historian Edward G. Lengel writes: "In two weeks, six hundred thousand men, four thousand guns, ninety thousand horses, and almost a million tons of supplies would move sixty miles from Saint-Mihiel to the Meuse-Argonne, and relieve 220,000 troops of the French Second Army." Across a front that stretched about fifteen miles, the Americans attacked with nine divisions abreast (in all, six hundred thousand troops), but immediately ran into trouble. In the first four days of the fighting, the U.S. Army suffered forty-five thousand casualties, and from a simple bike ride to Montfaucon I could see why. The road felt more like Sitting Duck Alley than any pathway for a successful attack against fortified lines.

For all that the American general staff preached the tactics of combined arms—infantry, artillery, and even air force—Black Jack Pershing was still of the belief that rifles and bayonets could carry the field. On October 19, 1917, he said optimistically (as is quoted in Lengel): "The rifle and bayonet remain the supreme weapons of the infantry soldier. The ultimate success of the army depends upon their proper use in open warfare."

Nevertheless, the terrain between Malancourt and Montfaucon is an unusual blend of open farmland and copses of dense woods, which gave the Germans perfect places to set up their machine guns and entrench their defenders. Montfaucon itself sits at the top of a long incline. From its heights, which now have the American memorial, the Germans could watch the American advance and pick them off as if at a shooting gallery. Nevertheless, in the stalled advance Pershing saw only a lack of drive on the part of his men. "Action is the first law of war," he liked to say. "Of all mistakes only one is disgraceful—inaction." In this case, "action" nearly wiped out an army.

What America Lost on the Western Front
Montfaucon to Romagne

IT WAS MIDAFTERNOON WHEN I RODE, very hungry, into
Montfaucon and found a hotel café mentioned in one of my
guidebooks. The owner brought me a beer and a large sandwich, which I ate at an outside table. He seemed pleased to
serve me, and we chatted about what I was doing and where
I was from. I explained that I was now living in Switzerland,
but that I had been born in New York. To illustrate how few
tourists now bother with the Meuse-Argonne theater, he said
cheerfully: "Really. Just two years ago we had another guest
from New York, and he, too, was on his bike."

I sipped my beer, studied my maps, ate dessert, filled
my water bottles, and drank coffee before setting off up the
last part of the hill, to the towering American memorial.
Built in the 1920s, the Doric column rises from the trees and
looks like the one on top of Bunker Hill in Boston. The purpose of the memorial is for visitors to climb the 234 wind-
ing stairs to the top and take in a commanding view of the
battlefield—the same one that the Germans used to claim
so many American casualties. I made the climb and took
pictures of the surroundings, remembering the words of
Marine Captain Lloyd Williams, who incarnated the wide-

spread American innocence about the war. Told to move his men back in an earlier battle, he retorted: "Retreat? Hell, we just got here."

I found this quotation in a history by Meirion and Susie Harries, *The Last Days of Innocence: America at War, 1917-1918*. I tracked down a copy when I was back home, because I had read and admired their work about the Japanese army, *Soldiers of the Sun: The Rise and Fall of the Imperial Japanese Army*. Their book about the United States in World War I is less about the actual battlefield engagements—although they are covered—than about the effects of the war on American society. They conclude: "During the First World War, a torrent of new phenomena overwhelmed the United States: a wash of public money flooding the economy; a hugely inflated federal government; universal conscription; a system for surveillance of the people; a pervasive suspicion and fear of the foreign and unorthodox; and then, with the rise of Bolshevism, a threatening alien ideology that seemed to justify the fears."

At the declaration of war in 1917, the United States was closer to Thomas Jefferson's pastoral affiliations than to today's Department of Homeland Security and the national surveillance state. Although it had defeated Spain in the colonial wars in Cuba and the Philippines, the army was small, and the preparations for foreign wars few. The Harrieses write: "The joke going around in Washington was that the General Staff knew so little about Germany that they were ransacking the plan drawer marked 'J' for a war plan." Local draft boards were set up, they recount, so that "men were not taken from their homes by the Army; they were delivered to the Army by their neighbors." They describe how, equally fancifully, "early antisubmarine officers were ordered to hit the periscope of an attacking submarine with a mallet."

Despite such quaint preparations for war, the Harrieses describe how "by the summer of 1918, coercion had replaced volunteerism as the mainspring of the war effort at home. . . . In the eyes of many liberals America was no longer a place of tolerance, openness, and democracy; it was divided, intolerant, vindictive, and submissive to the demands of a central authority that attempted to control people's lives down to the details of the food they ate, the newspapers they read, and the conversations they were permitted to hold in public. In the crucible of total war, the nation had lost its innocence; few could now claim with absolute conviction the moral superiority over the corrupt nations of the Old World that it had once possessed."

Nevertheless, the goal of President Woodrow Wilson's administration was to keep the American army under a separate command, away from European control, even though England and France had learned many painful lessons in over three years of trench warfare. Pershing stated (as is quoted in Lengel) that "the underlying idea must be kept in view that the forces of the United States are a separate and distinct component of the combined forces, the identity of which must be preserved."

The Harrieses write that the supreme allied commander, Marshal Ferdinand Foch, agreed with this request, in part because he was a wily and political French general and would do anything to get the Americans into the war on the side of the Allies. Meuse-Argonne would be the test of this formula and, at least for the Americans, would prove a disaster. The Harrieses write: "On September 2, Pershing committed the

First Army to the two-battle operation. To preserve the integrity of his army, he had placed the most horrifying burden on it. Why Foch had allowed him to do so is not quite clear. It was almost as though Foch, as a Frenchman rather than Supreme Commander, a politician as well as a soldier, was reluctant for the Americans to distinguish themselves, content to see them bite off more than they could chew."

I lingered atop the Montfaucon memorial and then descended to continue the ride north, through farmland and forest strongholds, to the heights around Cunel and Romagne. It is where some of the hardest fighting took place in the Argonne, and is now the location of the vast American cemetery. I needed to get there before it closed at 5 p.m., which meant pushing hard up the last hills into Cunel and turning left and gliding down into Romagne and the cemetery. I decided not to walk the bike around the cemetery, so I hid it behind some bushes and strolled the burial grounds of more than twelve thousand Americans.

My pictures of the cemetery show long rows of white crosses but none of the crowds that visit Verdun. For the most part I was alone, except for the sea of geometrically perfect rows of headstones, which at any angle look like soldiers, albeit dead ones, on parade. To be fair, Romagne is on the way to nowhere. Paris is a three-hour drive to the west, and Luxembourg is probably two hours to the northeast. That said, I found it sad that so few Americans abroad bother to come here, although in another sense, to use one of Lincoln's phrases in the Gettysburg Address, it is "altogether fitting" that the Meuse-Argonne is overlooked and forgotten. The Harrieses quote the reaction of one American soldier in France to the news that he gets from the homeland. He says:

"It will never do to let the people at home find out the truth about this war. They've been fed on bunk until they'd never believe anything that didn't sound like a monk's story of the Crusades. Every time I get a paper from home, I either break into a loud laugh or get mad."

Nor does the cemetery quote the words of isolationist senator George Norris of Nebraska, who spoke out against the war, which would eventually cost $10 billion (that's in 1918 currency) and 75,658 killed either in the fighting or the great influenza pandemic. In opposing the declaration of war, Norris said (as quoted by the Harries): "I feel we are committing a sin against humanity and against our countrymen. I would say to this war god: You shall not coin into gold the lifeblood of my brethren. . . . I feel that we are about to put the dollar sign upon the American flag."

Lorraine in the Mist
Montmédy to Sedan

From Romagne I took a road north that angled toward the river, figuring I would make better time along the Meuse than if I continued through the hills to Sedan. I also needed a place to stay for the night. On my maps, towns such as Dun-sur-Meuse and Stenay looked more promising for hotels than anything I saw in the hills before Sedan. The weather remained glorious. There was no wind, and I had the setting sun at my back.

The road to Dun was up and down, as if I were riding on long ocean rollers, although the sea in this case was broad, open farmland that would have been kind to the attacking Americans once they punched through the heights of Romagne and Cunel. Harder to find, however, was a hotel. In Dun I saw what looked like summer camping grounds, but no hotels. That led me to ride on toward Stenay, where the perfect day of biking gave way to an interminable stretch of national highway, with heavy truck traffic and tight shoulders. A few times I stood in the grass to let a car or truck go past. Now, with the wind in my face, I got to Stenay only as it was beginning to get dark.

Perhaps in summer Stenay has qualities that draws tourists—one brochure spoke of "flora and fauna, concerts, boutiques, and water sports"—but I could see little that was attractive as I biked around the empty center in search of a hotel. Finally I found one on a road heading toward the river. The manager said, yes, he had a room, and gave me the key. He also said that he was going home and that I would be the only guest in the building that night. He wasn't fussed about storing my bike in a closet, and he pointed to a little restaurant where I could find dinner. Then he was off, leaving me to soak in the tub before I ate spaghetti at a small café. Back in the room, I fell asleep in my clothes, tired from the sixty miles on the bike.

The next morning, with nothing for breakfast at the hotel and the town apparently closed until noon, I had the last of my roadside apples and set off for Montmédy, mentioned in one of my guides as a town with an impressive medieval fortress. (In the Napoleonic wars, it held out for three months after the defeat at Waterloo.) From there I could also catch the train to Sedan, as I no longer wanted any part of the truck traffic on D 964.

On the map, Montmédy looked only about ten miles away, although it was more than that with the hills and some wrong turns that I made in the dense morning fog. Lorraine was socked in, and in a few stretches of the road I decided to wait on the side until the traffic had cleared. If yesterday's sunshine had been the last day of summer, today was the first day of fall. I took no pleasure, on an empty stomach and no coffee, chuffing up steep hills in the fog, trying to find my way to a fortress that, while it could be interesting, was only a waypoint on my road to Sedan.

Inside Montmédy fortress is a small village of houses and a hotel, although the latter was closed, so that wasn't an option for my late breakfast. After inspecting the ramparts, which were indeed medieval and came with some draw-bridges, I rode down into the modern town and hunted around for a café. The choices all looked terrible. One was a gambling parlor that served coffee and sandwiches shrink-wrapped in plastic. Another was a bar that didn't have food, although by then I was thinking about a beer. Finally I settled on a small *boulangerie* that had tables, cof-fee, and, of course, quiche Lorraine. I had, to use the Monty Python expression, "the lot," and ate while staring at a map of Sedan, trying to figure out how I might see the contours of the battle that settled the Franco-Prussian War, at least its early phases near Metz.

Between 1871 and 1919, recovering the lost provinces of Alsace and Lorraine was the French national obsession. (Guedalla writes: "For France yielded Alsace (except Belfort), a great part of Lorraine including Metz, and five milliards [billions] of francs, the bitter price of making war with insuf-ficient preparation.") A famous painting of the era depicts a schoolteacher showing his class a map of France. There is a black stain, presumably one of shame, where Alsace and Lor-raine should be. Now that Lorraine is part of France, how-ever, it seems as though it has been left out in the cold. Maybe it worked better as an adjustment claim in Franco-German relations?

"As for me," the celebrated French thinker Remy de Gourmont wrote on the eve of World War I, "I wouldn't give the little finger of my right hand for those forgotten prov-inces. My hand needs it to rest on as I write. Nor would I give the little finger of my left hand. I need it to flick the ash from my cigarette."

Waiting in the fog on the Montmédy platform for the train to Sedan, I was shivering from the dampness. A train headlamp emerged from the murk, and I rode twenty minutes into Sedan, by which time the mist had burned away.

Before looking for the scenes of battle or what remains of them, I decided to bike into the town center and find the tourist office—nearly every French town has one—and see if it might have a map of the memorials. The office, however, was closed on the Monday. The hours posted made visiting Sedan sound like something that needed to fit the rigid schedule of the local civil service.

I studied maps on the walls of the tourist office and my photocopied pages from Michael Howard's book that showed where the battle was fought and where Napoleon III had surrendered to Bismarck and the kaiser. A Bismarck biographer, Edward Crankshaw, describes the context: "It was the last time in history that a soldier-king, a monarch, was to stand on a hill-top and look down on the battlefield; it was the first time as well as the last that a civilian prime minister sat watching the progress of the battle he brought about, while dictating telegrams dealing with its aftermath."

Sedan is an odd mixture of a historic regional city and a place where garish pizza joints pipe music into the street. A medieval citadel looms over the center square, a city on the French frontier. The decaying fortress feels like the core of a dead volcano around which are the hills of the Franco-Prussian War. Of the Emperor's last retreat, his biographer Graham Brooks writes in the *Great Lives* series:

> So began the tragic trek which was to end in Sedan. For days the peasantry of eastern France were treated to their

first glimpse of the Emperor; they saw a pale and haggard figure, bent with pain, crouched in the corner of his carriage and jolting along the dusty roads in the wake of his army, asserting no authority, ignored by the officers and jeered at by the men, gazing with lacklustre eyes into to future and waiting for the end – the pitiful wreck of what had once been Naopleon III.

Before striking out, and hoping for more sun, I drank coffee and sat on a terrace that looked up at the ramparts. Not many people were about, as this was a late September weekday morning. When I asked directions toward Floing, my first stop, the waitress shrugged, as though I had sought her views on why Marshal MacMahon and the emperor had taken the remnants of the French army to this cul-de-sac in Lorraine. One hypothesis is that—with Bazaine locked up in Metz—they were thinking that, come the worst, they could lead the army across the border into neutral Luxembourg.

Another suggestion is that Sedan had qualities of a redoubt that would be difficult for the Germans to attack. Wawro writes: "The need to avoid the oncoming Germans and feed his hungry armies impelled MacMahon northward where the roads climbed steeply through forested defiles and there was only one overtaxed railway." The German military commander Helmuth von Moltke said: "Now we have them in a mousetrap." In the end, however, the best description of the situation came from the French general A. A. Ducrot, who said: "We are in the chamber pot and there we shall be crapped upon." (In French it sounds more poetic: *"Nous sommes dan un pot du chambre, et nous y serons emmerdés."*) He proved correct.

— 54 —

Napoleon III Loses it Around Sedan
Donchery

MY ROUTE FOR THE DAY was a ten-to fifteen-mile loop around the contours of Sedan, going clockwise from Floing to Illy, Givonne, Daigny, La Moncelle, and Bazeilles, where the most intense action took place in the one-day battle of September 2, 1870. The French marshal MacMahon had deployed his men around the crown of the Sedan hillside. There they waited for the German attacks. Instead of rushing the entrenched lines, as at Gravelotte, the Germans sat back and blasted the French lines, turning the day into short work for the artillery and forcing the emperor to surrender his army. Wawro writes: "Sedan was another victory for Moltke's operational art and Prussian tactics. It was, as an Austro-Hungarian officer later wrote, 'an artillery battle par excellence.'"

In each village on the outskirts of Sedan where the battle was contested, I stopped in the town square to read the plaques and consult my maps. Mostly I enjoyed the ride, which was on a small agricultural road that during the fighting had delineated the front line between the Germans and the French. By now the fog had lifted and the sun was warming the air. Cows were feeding in many of the pastures, and the villages struck me as more prosperous than those around Montmédy.

I especially liked the landscape around Illy, where steam from the wet grass glistened in the morning sunshine. To my right, up the hillside, I imagined the French dug into their positions, while on my left, down the hill, the Germans would have deployed their artillery. In theory, the French should have held out longer than a day, but they had no answer for the accurate long-range German artillery. Wawro credits the German victory to the "effectiveness of the Prussian guns." He goes on to cite the casualties in just one day:

> 3,000 French dead, 14,000 French wounded, and 21,000 French prisoners against a total of 9,000 German dead, wounded, and missing. Sedan was an altogether different battle from Gravelotte, where German and French casualties had been equal; here the French lost at the rate of four-to-one, an unsustainable ratio. Watching the slaughter with Bismarck and Moltke on the height of Frénois, the American observer Phil Sheridan wondered how Napoleon III would survive it: "Oh no," Bismarck chortled. "The old fox is too cunning to be caught in such a trap; he has doubtless slipped off to Paris."

Owing to a painful kidney stone, Napoleon III could hardly slip on or off his horse, let alone vanish to Paris. By the end of the day, to end the slaughter, he had no choice but to offer the kaiser his sword. No photographs were taken of the surrender, but numerous paintings have survived. Nearly all show Kaiser Wilhelm I with Bismarck and Moltke, each wearing full military dress and pointed pickelhaube helmets, standing proudly while the emperor grovels to get a cease-fire. The picture of Napoleon III seated on a bench in Donchery was drawn to make him look like a beggar, as perhaps by then he was. From Sedan, he abdicated his throne and was sent to prison in Cassel, Germany.

Edward Crankshaw, a Bismarck biographer, describes the burlesque of the emperor heading into exile. He writes:

> All the imperial baggage wagons and carriages stood drawn up ready for the road; the French household appeared in their well-known rich liveries, even the postilions were in gala dress, and powdered, 'as though for a trip to the races at Longjumeau.'

Bismarck took particular pleasure in the humiliation of the French emperor. "It was agreed that he should go to Cassel," writes Guedalla, "where the captive Emperor had asked for the company of his three captive Marshals. Bismarck remarked irreverently that Napoleon appeared to want a game of whist."

The small museum in Bezeilles was closed, and when I asked around in Balan, a suburb, if anyone knew the place where Marshal MacMahon had been wounded, the reactions I got indicated that it was not a pressing community issue.

In early afternoon I was back in Sedan. I could not find a restaurant that I liked or one from which I could easily watch my bike. I ended up picking up the ingredients of a picnic and eating in a park before catching the train to Mézières— the elusive goal of the American Meuse-Argonne offensive in 1918.

By the end of the war on November 11, 1918, the American advance had reached only to Stenay, where I had spent the night before as the sole guest in the forlorn hotel. The politics at the end of the Great War around Sedan were as complicated as those that surrounded the emperor's abdication in 1870. In the Franco-Prussian War, the French government collapsed after Sedan, leading to more fighting and the Paris commune.

In 1918, not only did the Argonne offensive fail to reach the Sedan-Mézières rail line, but the weight of the American attack ended any German illusions that President Wilson could, as he had promised, arbitrate a just peace as an honest broker. The Harrieses write: "Now complete humiliation was but a few days away—at the hands of the Americans, in whose President the Germans had placed their hopes for a fair peace."

Marshal Pétain Devours His Own

Reims

FROM SEDAN, the Franco-Prussian War shifted to Paris, visiting which was also my plan, but first I decided to stop off in Reims and see the cathedral.

The city was bathed in sunshine as I biked around on the cobblestones, although without a bike lock all I could do at the cathedral was to stand inside the entrance until one of the guards shooed me away. I didn't mind, as I preferred to be outside in the shade of some nearby trees, where I drank an afternoon coffee at a café and read *Dare Call It Treason* by Richard M. Watt, a history of the 1917 French army mutinies that began in the trenches not far from Reims.

The book I had in my saddlebag dealt with the near collapse of the French army after Verdun, when troops in the lines for the attacks at Chemin des Dames mutinied against their commanders, notably General Nivelle, who had moved up from his day-to-day command at Verdun (after May 1916) to lead French forces on the Western Front in 1917. As he did at Verdun, Nivelle squandered the lives of his men with useless attacks into the meat grinders.

At Chemin des Dames the troops were of no mind to go over the top one more time for Nivelle. They mutinied, forcing the French high command to turn, again, to Marshal

Pétain to restore order. He did so, although in the suppression he ordered many men shot who were not guilty of insubordination. Watt writes: "The true horror of World War I was not in its maimed and killed, nor in the length of the war, and not in its barbarism or atrocities—it was in the fact that *so many men died and achieved nothing for it.* And no nation suffered proportionately more than France."

More than an account of the mutinies, Watt's book is a history of French military politics between 1870 and 1918, when so much of its doctrine focused on élan and orders to move forward with the bayonet. (A popular expression was: "The French soldier can do anything with a bayonet except sit on it.") Watt summarizes the mentality that ruled the French army at the outbreak of war in 1914:

> If all went as scheduled, the signal for the attack would be given, the bands would play and the ardent infantry would dash forward shouting "Vive la France!" and "A la baïonnette!" and fling itself upon a German foe stunned by the *élan* of their enemy. Through the gaps torn by the vicious bayonet attacks of the infantry, the cavalry would charge to saber or lance down the fleeing Hun. Such, anyhow, was the plan.

Little wonder that France lost more than two million men in the first two years of the fighting. Even French casualties were a measure of the army's bizarre logic. Watt writes: "If losses were high, then the attack, however otherwise fruitless, could be represented as having been 'pressed home with vigor and *élan*.' If the losses were light, then, somehow, it was thought that the troops had 'failed in their duty.' Even wholesale losses could be interpreted as victories, of a sort."

He continues: "The staff officers at G.Q.G. have even invented a name for it; they call it 'maintaining moral ascendancy.' The pursuance of this precept cost the French Army about 1,500 casualties a day."

At Verdun, as Pétain's successor commanding the French Second Army, Nivelle maintained moral ascendancy at the cost of thousands of lives. Watt writes: "Nevertheless, for a battle which started out as fundamentally an artillery engagement on a vast scale, Verdun speedily degenerated into a succession of wild infantry melees which were distinguished only by the vast numbers of troops who died and by the valor displayed on both sides. . . . Fresh divisions were fed into the battle, remained in action for a few days and emerged from Verdun grotesque fractions of their previous strength."

A year later, not far from Reims at Chemin des Dames, Nivelle's plan was so flawed that the outgoing minister of defense compared it (as quoted in Watt) to "the sort that one would expect to have dreamed up 'the army of the Grand Duchess of Gerolstein.'" Men rebelled because they were sent back to the front lines when it wasn't "their turn" to go forward again. Watt writes that the mutinies spread because:

First, aside from the failure of the Nivelle offensive and the crushing blow which this dealt the troops' morale, there were a vast number of subordinate military factors which entered into the picture. The miserable "rest" camps, the lack of leave, the picture of G.Q.G. which had grown up in the men's minds as a distant, indifferent monster, neither knowing about nor caring for the troops who must pay for its errors with their lives—all these bore heavily on the troops' unrest.

Only when Pétain, in response, took to randomly shoot-ing innocent soldiers did the revolts subside, although he also worked to improve conditions behind the lines for the men. The mutinies also explain why Foch was willing to agree to a separate American command structure in 1917, if that was what it took to get fresh divisions into the depleted lines.

As much as I wanted to see the trenches at Chemin des Dames, I could not work out how to get there by bike and train, and then on to Paris. Besides, I had seen many trenches around Verdun. Instead, I chose to have an afternoon glass of champagne in Épernay, also close to Reims, and then to catch a train to Paris, where I would spend several days washing my clothes and tracking down Franco-Prussian artifacts around the city.

In particular, I wanted to go the Clemenceau Museum, as Georges Clemenceau was another link between 1870 and 1917, when he was appointed prime minister to bring the war to its bloody conclusion. Nicknamed "the Tiger" for an iras-cible personality that had him fighting with everyone, Clem-enceau said bluntly, "I wage war." He also said, perhaps with Nivelle in mind, that "war is too important to be left to the soldiers."

The Second Imperial Act
Closes Out of Town
Around Paris

I NEVER QUITE MASTERED BIKING AROUND PARIS, although I found I had little choice but to ride with abandon on the avenues, as other cyclists would come up behind me—just like the cars—and ring little bells for me to move faster or get out of their way.

Paris does have a network of cycling lanes, as well as a fleet of shared bicycles, but the code of the streets is more chaotic than it appears on the brochures about the rise of the Parisian bike culture. Because I now had a decent lock, I could park my bike outside museums and cafés, making the city more accessible than if I were getting around on the Metro or by foot. Even at night I would go out for rides, enjoying the narrow streets or the Île Saint-Louis after rush hour traffic had subsided.

I did not confine myself to Franco-Prussianism in Paris. I signed up for a walking tour of Talleyrand's ministry and saw a movie about the repression of civil rights in Iran. I ate a number of good meals with my cousin Stanislav Stanojević, a filmmaker, who adjusted to my habits of getting around on the bike.

I started in Paris at Clemenceau's apartment, now a museum, on the rue Franklin, which in a small square also has a statue of the good doctor—seated sternly in bronze as opposed to his more familiar pose, that of charming the ladies at a Paris levee.

Clemenceau escaped the obscurity of most Third Republic politicians by coming to power with a coalition government in 1917 and serving through the end of the Great War and the signing of the Treaty of Versailles. (He left office in 1920.) He did, as he said, "wage war." He was ruthless in imposing a harsh peace on the Germans at Versailles, or as the phrase had it, "making the Hun pay." He had first been elected to office in Paris in 1871, during the humiliations that followed Sedan. In many ways his political career can be read as a long denunciation of German arrogance, which he repaid with the same coin. Nevertheless, he was not part of the negotiations in January 1871 that cast such a pall over Franco-German relations for the next seventy years.

* * *

To pick up the story after Napoleon III and his whist partners departed for prison in Germany, the surrender of Sedan on September 2, 1870, left Bazaine with the only army in France capable of fighting the Germans, and he was bottled up in Metz. The marshal did make some halfhearted attempts to break the siege, but his heart wasn't in the fight. Wawro writes:

> For the successful defense of Paris, Metz was still the key.
> It contained 135,000 professional troops with 600 guns,
> three marshals of France, fifty generals, and 6,000 offi-

cers. Bazaine had somehow to extricate this force and maneuver to relieve Paris either with his own army or with new armies that could be formed and trained by his professional cadres.

Instead of fighting his way out of Metz, Bazaine sanctioned a bizarre diplomatic mission to England, in which the emperor's wife, Eugenie, then in exile in Hastings, entered into negotiations with Prussian envoys. The proposal was that Bazaine be allowed to depart Metz with his army and, under Prussian supervision, put down the riots then engulfing Paris and its new revolutionary government. Wawro writes:

> If the mission succeeded, if they won the race with time and German magnanimity conceded a reasonable peace to a restored Empire, Bazaine would be judged to have struck a good bargain for his country. But since the Germans are not magnanimous and the event showed that France was no longer Bonapartist, it failed completely, leaving him to face the indignation of all French republicans and royalists. Bazaine had guessed wrong; but there is a difference between error and treason.

The hope was that the Prussians had as much at stake in the French monarchy as did Napoleon and Eugenie or, failing that, in a government with Bazaine at the head. If you are going to *faire Kamerad* to get a better deal, you might as well surrender an army and not just yourself. The negotiations went nowhere. Bazaine was obliged to surrender Metz to the Germans, and later he was convicted of treason. "At last Bazaine and MacMahon have joined forces," Parisians joked darkly.

Although German armies moved from Sedan and Metz to surround Paris, and shelled the city from nearby hills, the main action there was diplomatic, with Bismarck maneuvering to impose severe conditions on the French, even though his counterpart in the peace negotiations was a makeshift coalition government that included Léon Gambetta. Bismarck was determined to use his victory over France to unify Germany. For that, he needed to annex Alsace and part of Lorraine—to humiliate the French and bind together northern and southern Germany, under Prussian rule. He said (as is quoted in Wawro): "It is a mistake to count upon 'gratitude,' especially the 'gratitude' of a nation. . . . Over the past 200 years France has declared war on Prussia thirty times and . . . you will do so again; for that we must be prepared, with . . . a territorial glacis between you and us."

Wawro writes that the "armistice terms that Bismarck offered the French, though severe, were not excessive given France's instigation of the war. The Prussians would end the siege of Paris and declare the war at an end if the French would cede Alsace and half Lorraine, pay the Prussian war costs, and yield the Parisian forts of Valérien and St. Denis until the indemnity was paid." Nevertheless, the French refused.

Not even the presence in Paris of American Civil War general Ambrose Burnside as President Grant's envoy could persuade Jules Favre to negotiate with the Germans. As recounted by Wawro, Favre, France's new foreign minister, told Bismarck, "We are the government of national defense. You know what our program is: 'Not a clod of our earth or a stone of our fortresses.'" The Germans resumed the shelling of Paris until France relented, and a peace was signed at Versailles. Wawro describes the process:

Cheated in 1866, Roon and Moltke bore down at Versailles and secured 5 billion francs ($15 billion today), Lorraine up to Metz and Thionville, all of Alsace, and a victory parade through the streets of Paris. Bismarck, who had led the "anti-Metz faction" at Versailles, quite uncharacteristically wilted under the pressure: "The soldiers will not hear of giving up Metz, and perhaps they are right."

The ceremony in the Hall of Mirrors was calculated to humiliate France, the Versailles palace and salle des glaces having been constructed 200 years earlier by Louis XIV, whose military campaigns had shattered Germany into the impotent statelets that were only now being unified by Bismarck.

Even at the time, the reactions to the peace were similar to those later heard following the 1919 Treaty of Versailles. Wawro quotes the *Economist* magazine in March 1871, that "to exact huge sums of money as the consequence of victory suggests a belief that money may next time be the object as well as the actual reward of battle. A flavor of huckstering is introduced into the relations between States." He goes on: "Einheit – unity – was achieved at the expense of Freiheit – freedom. The German Empire became, in Karl Marx's words, 'a military despotism cloaked in parliamentary forms with a feudal ingredient, influenced by the bourgeoisie, festooned with bureaucrats and guarded by police.'"

Bismarck later asserted that taking Alsace was "an idea of the professors," but his biographer Crankshaw writes, "He needed this slice of the Rhineland as the cement to hold North and South Germany together." He added that Bismarck's policies transformed the conflict "from a war of professional armies into a national war of survival and revenge. The marvelous victory was tarnished, its splendor never to be recovered." Crown Prince Friedrich put it more bluntly at the end of 1870: "Bismarck has made us great and powerful, but he has robbed us of our friends, the sympathies of the world, and—our conscience."

Georges Clemenceau Has the Last Word
Versailles

EVEN THOUGH IN MY TRAVELS I was coming to the opinion that Clemenceau was an unpleasant man, I could have spent hours at his house and museum. He led a long, event-filled, complicated political life, and many objects from his household downstairs are now in the museum on the second floor.

Moving through the glass cabinets of his life, I saw photographs of his American wife, Mary Plummer (whom he treated poorly), his dueling pistols (for which he had occasional use), sketches depicting his role in breaking up the Paris commune (with cannons on top of Montmartre), the numerous books and articles that he wrote (professionally he was a journalist, not a lawyer), copies of newspapers about the Dreyfus affair (he and Émile Zola helped acquit the unjustly imprisoned officer Alfred Dreyfus), pictures of his visits to the troops on the front lines (and in a ticker tape parade in New York City), and posters of his legacy (a group in Arizona started the Bank of Clemenceau).

Not surprisingly, in the museum there are no pictures of Clemenceau at Versailles with President Woodrow Wilson, whom he found insufferable. Clemenceau said famously to Wilson's adviser: "I understand you but talking to Wilson is something like talking to Jesus Christ." When Wilson presented his Fourteen Points to Congress in January 1919, Clemenceau remarked: "God only needed ten."

The apartment where he lived is still as Clemenceau left it when he died in 1929. No other tenants lived there, and his furniture was made part of the museum soon after he died. His routine was to get up at 5 a.m., work at the desk next to his bed, exercise with a physical trainer, and then at 8:45 a.m. head to the ministry. For most of his political career he was out of power, as his specialty in the Third Republic was to bring down governments. Nasty opposition came to him naturally. A colleague in the National Assembly said about him: "M. Clemenceau's words are like cold, sharp, well-tempered steel and his speeches resemble fencing-matches in which his direct lunges pierce his adversaries."

Once back from my trip, I read several biographies of the Tiger, the best being *George Clemenceau: A Political Biography* by David Robin Watson, which deals less with his marriage and mistresses and more with his parliamentary maneuverings that brought down so many governments. He does describe his birth in 1837 in the Vendée, a region of western France where he later kept a country home, and his evolution from medical studies to journalism.

Clemenceau was fluent in English, and in the 1860s he was working as a French teacher in Stamford, Connecticut, when he met his future wife, Mary. He married her in 1869 and presently moved back to France, where after a while he shunned her and took on a series of lovers. When much later she did the same, he pounced on the chance to divorce her. She never returned to America, and late in her life could be seen around Paris, earning small amounts of money explaining points of interest in English to American tourists.

After a stint in Parisian politics, Clemenceau was elected to the Chamber of Deputies in 1876, where he would remain, on and off, until after World War I. His contrarian personality had him in shifting alliances with the far left or right, depending on who was in power. Only once before the national crisis of 1917 was he asked to form a ministry, which, like many he had trashed, promptly fell from power. After 1870, France suffered from political stalemate for more than a generation. Watson writes: "The Senate was to the end of the Third Republic the instrument by which the rural areas exercised a veto over the whole political machine."

Other than his permanent opposition and devotion to biting wit, Clemenceau had no firm convictions as a political man, moving from liberalism to conservatism as he grew older. He did, however, define himself by his enemies, and an early one was Otto von Bismarck, of whom he said: "Bismarck is a dangerous enemy, but even more dangerous perhaps as a friend: he showed us Tunis, placing us in conflict with England, and is now negotiating with us over the Congo."

Clemenceau would remain suspicious about Germany during his entire career. In the 1880s he flirted with the comic political figure General Ernest Boulanger—who stood for *revanche* (revenge against Germany), *révision* (revision of the Constitution), *et restoration* (a return of the monarchy)— until eventually Clemenceau turned on the man (on horseback) who wanted to save France from dissolution.

In the late nineteenth century, when Clemenceau was out of the Assembly, he teamed with the novelist Émile Zola to publish denunciations (such as the famous *J'accuse*) of Alfred Dreyfus's false conviction and imprisonment. Clemenceau was a rebel with many causes, although happiest when he could say *non* to whomever was in power.

* * *

CLEMENCEAU WAS CHOSEN to form a government in 1917 because three years of war had discredited most other leading politicians, all of whom could count on Clemenceau only for snide opposition. Much like Winston Churchill in the 1930s, he never thought French governments were doing enough to prosecute the war. Watson writes: "For more than three years his contribution to the war effort was as an unflagging critic of a succession of cabinets, most of them headed by prime ministers he cordially despised—Viviani, Briand, Ribot, Painlevé." He called Aristide Briand "the *chef d'orchestre* of defeatism," much as ten years later he said, "Poincaré and Foch gave me more trouble than the anarchists."

Clemenceau was brought to power because, Watson writes, "When those who had governed France during the first three years of the war became discredited, Clemenceau stood out as the one political figure who had challenged them by demanding a more vigorous conduct of the war, not from a left-wing position based on illusory hopes of a compromise peace."

Unlike his predecessors, Clemenceau had the good fortune to take office when the Americans were sending a million men to France, and when Germany was willing to gamble everything on an ill-advised 1918 spring offensive. When Russia was forced to quit the alliance and the war, he said (as is quoted in Watson): "Let us keep the moral advantage of being betrayed." At the Paris Peace Conference, he went it alone, dismissive of his subordinates, not to mention the Allies. He said of his finance minister, Louis-Lucien Klotz:

"Just my luck to get hold of the only Jew who can't count." He asked another aide to tell him who was this Stephen Pichon standing before him. When told he was France's foreign minister, Clemenceau replied: "So he is. I had forgotten it."

Any time Woodrow Wilson appeared in view, Clemenceau must have rolled his eyes. (He said: "I like the League. I just don't believe in it.") He did, however, believe in punishing Germany in the peace as Bismarck had done to France in 1870. The U.S. envoy at Versailles, William Bullitt, said, "This isn't a peace treaty. I can see at least eleven wars in it." He was referring to Clemenceau's insistence that Germany be made to suffer. When British prime minister David Lloyd George got back to Britain and was asked how he had done at the peace conference, he said: "Not badly, considering I was seated between Jesus Christ and Napoleon."

After the war, Clemenceau took a victory lap around the United States, thanks to his American friend, Wilson's adviser Colonel Edward House, who arranged speaking engagements and hotels in Boston, New York, Pittsburgh, Chicago, and St. Louis. In Washington, Clemenceau met President Warren Harding in the White House and later was quoted in the *New York Times*: "Oh, we talked a lot about Napoleon and some other things as well."

Watson writes that "in the autumn of 1922 he undertook a lecture tour of the United States, speaking in all the major cities of the northeast. His theme was defense of French policy, especially with regard to war-debts and Reparations, and condemnation of the American withdrawal from the alliance." By then, however, Germany had gone to the revolutionary and monetary wall, and Adolf Hitler was plotting his beer-hall putsch.

General Boulanger Falls Off
His Hobby Horse
Paris

My readings about Clemenceau got me interested in General Ernest Boulanger, but I was at a loss as to where I could go in Paris to learn more about him. On my ride in the Argonne, after leaving Montfaucon, I had stopped at the small village of Nantillois, where at the crossroads there is a large memorial to the Pennsylvania 80th Division and a small statue on a pedestal of Boulanger, who is identified only as minister of the Colonies and senator for the Meuse. The senator's bust makes it look as though someone had punched him in the left eye. Perhaps the husband of one of his lovers?

In Paris, I could not locate a museum dedicated to his life or even another statue. I knew the outlines of his career: He was born in Brittany and did army service in North Africa and Indochina before 1870. During the war he served bravely and was promoted to colonel. Later he became a general and was appointed a government minister, at which time an adoring following sprang up around his somewhat vapid persona.

To many across the political spectrum, Boulanger was thought to represent a way out of the political stalemate that saw governments fall frequently and the Germans still occupying Lorraine and Alsace. To those on the right, he stood for revenge against the Germans and the restoration of the monarchy. Those on the left saw him as an alternative to the weak governments that never remained long in power. Ordinary citizens believed he stood for law and order. In my travels, however, Boulanger remained a blank slate, much like his actual state of mind.

I decided my best chance to see a picture of the general or learn more about him was at the Musée de l'Armée (Army Museum), located in the great complex at Les Invalides, which includes the tomb of Napoleon Bonaparte. After all, Boulanger had achieved his fame, or cult status, as a general, and he had commanded troops in the colonial army, not to mention outside Paris in the Franco-Prussian War. Fortunately, Les Invalides is easy to find on a bike; it's near the river Seine and surrounded with open spaces.

In tracking down the general, I headed directly for the collections dealing with the events of 1870 and beyond. I found numerous swords, uniforms, saddles, and pistols, but nothing that mentioned Boulanger. I did find a large portrait of Napoleon III—he looks like the headwaiter at a hotel in Cannes, with a red jacket and a wispy Vandyke beard—and some excellent paintings of the fighting in the Franco-Prussian War. About General Boulanger there was nothing. I should not have been surprised, as he stands for those generals who would be king. His life and career are summed up in his failure to execute a successful coup d'état—not something to be remembered in the army museum.

I had better luck at my beloved Shakespeare and Company, the famous English-language bookstore in Paris, where

I found a copy of *The Astonishing Adventure of General Boulanger* by James Harding. Few books exist in English about the life of the amorous general, and this biography has the additional advantage of being detailed, well-written, and amusing. Harding's conclusion about the strange cult of "Boulangism" is that it was projected onto the general much in the same way Chance the Gardener is reborn as Chauncey Gardiner in the movie *Being There*.

In all aspects of his life, except for his naked ambition, Boulanger was mediocre. Harding quotes from one of his army fitness reports, which concludes: "An excellent officer, active, very intelligent, but ill-bred." A diplomat in Tunis, where Boulanger was stationed, wrote: "The General has more energy than intelligence. He needed it to reach the position he holds at his age, but he lacks a cultivated mind. He has no conversation, either. You feel that here is a man who has read little, thought little about higher things and who has no wide-ranging ideas. His whole mind is directed toward advancement and personal politics."

Like Woody Allen's Zelig, Boulanger's talent was to allow his personality to take on whatever characteristics his admirers desired. Harding describes a trip that he made in 1881 to the United States, to celebrate the one hundredth anniversary of the Battle of Yorktown, which required him to make the rounds in full military dress. "It was in America," writes Harding,

> that Boulanger might be said to have had his first taste of Boulangism. The crowds who assembled at various functions were stirred by his presence, and, without knowing anything of his character or background, cheered him in frenzies of blind enthusiasm.

In France, Harding writes: "The Royalists saw in Boulanger their King; Republicans saw their Republic; imperialists, their Caesar; patriots, the return of Metz and Strasbourg; peaceful folk saw order; and those who were restless saw an adventure which would solve all of their problems." Even the Tiger had a hand in launching his political career. According to Harding, Boulanger had done "all that Clemenceau had wanted of him. But the apprentice was soon to alarm the sorcerer who had conjured him onto the stage." Bismarck appreciated the general's personality, stating: "I didn't create Boulanger but he was very useful to me."

With women, especially the wives of his fellow officers, Boulanger found his true calling. Harding writes: "Women who were incautious enough to visit the General in his office discovered that agility and a mastery of tactics were useful attributes. A Polish countess, it was said, once had to fight a determined rearguard action in the Minister's study."

At critical times in his political career, when his supporters thought that, finally, the general would act for France, he was nowhere to be found and had gone off with a lover. Throughout the biography, Boulanger is always renting discreet apartments near his quarters, as Harding writes, to "transact business." Eventually he falls in love with Marguerite de Bonnemains (literally Margaret Goodhands). Harding describes the arrangement:

> The lovers rented a flat in the faubourg Saint-Honoré and Marguerite furnished it as a place for their meetings. The walls were lined with quilted pink silk, and the windows, of stained glass, were hung with thick curtains. Divans

and cushions were scattered about between antique church cupboards, gilt flambeaux and scent-burners. The flat resembled that luxurious, well-mirrored establishment in the rue Chabanais where prime ministers of the Third Republic often solved the government crises with the expert aid of beautiful young hostesses.[2]

However buffoonish Boulanger might appear, he represents a close call in French politics with a military coup d'état. Watt writes in his history that spans 1870 to 1917: "Boulangism (already it had a name) was a strange phenomenon. Strange because no one, perhaps least of all Boulanger, had a very clear idea where he stood or what he stood for. . . . Such was the confusion that among his supporters were Bonapartists, royalists, republicans, nationalists and even anarchists."

The confusion about his real political identity existed right up to the end, when he went into exile after a failed attempt by his supporters to push him to seize power. His best chance came on January 27, 1889, but he dithered at the moment of decision and rushed off to the arms of his lover. Shortly after a warrant for his arrest was issued, he fled the country, or, as one observer put it: "He skipped off like a pimp."

Boulanger went to Jersey, London, and finally Brussels, where in 1891 he shot himself in the head over the tombstone of Madame de Bonnemains. A famous 1891 magazine cover of *Le Petit Journal* shows a sketch of him in the cemetery,

---

2: A footnote to the passage reads: "Government hospitality was also extended to kings and others on state visits. Their calls at the Rue Chabanais always featured in the official circular as: 'Visit to the President of the Senate.'"

pointing a gun to his temple and, the reader may assume, to Boulangism. Always uneasy that he had nurtured such an erratic flame, Clemenceau sniffed: "Boulanger died, as he lived, as a subaltern."

Disguising Talleyrand as a Woman
Hotel Matignon

WHILE IN PARIS I FOLLOWED UP on an advertisement in *Le Monde* for a walking tour of the Hotel Matignon at 57 rue de Varenne. I decided to join, even though it was slightly off the beaten trail of the period between the Franco-Prussian War and World War I.

Waiting at the front gate at the appointed hour were about thirty people, many of them elderly women. We each paid ten euros to the guide, who wrote our names on a list and told us to wait in front of the palace. Although located on a nondescript alley in a crowded part of the city, the building is magnificent. Out the back is a large formal garden, where we could sit when the tour ended. We followed the guide from room to room, hearing about the furnishings, the architecture, and, what interested me most, what happened here when Talleyrand (his full name was Charles Maurice de Talleyrand-Périgord) owned it, from 1808 to 1811, and ran Napoleon I's complicated foreign affairs from a small room off the back garden. In 1820 the ministry of foreign affairs moved to the Quai d'Orsay, where it has been ever since.

I paid the most attention when the guide was speaking about the complicated relationship between Napoleon and Talleyrand, as the latter began his career as the bishop of

Autun (near Burgundy) and held important diplomatic posts during the *ancien régime*, the Revolution, and the restoration. He was more accommodating to power than Clemenceau was later, although both had a razor-sharp wit that could get them into trouble. He said (as is quoted by Talleyrand's biographer Duff Cooper) of his later rival Chateaubriand, "He only thinks he is deaf because he can no longer hear anyone talking about him." And he described Élie, duke of Decazes, as resembling "a fairly good-looking barber's assistant." Because of his travels and occasional exiles, he knew many in European and American politics, including Benedict Arnold, Aaron Burr, Thomas Jefferson, and Alexander Hamilton.

Talleyrand was an odd fit in the Revolution's Directory. Mirabeau said of him: "The Abbé de Périgord would sell his soul for money; and he would be right, for he would be exchanging dung for gold." Cooper gives an inkling of his powers of accommodating when it suited him. He writes: "A report that in his [Mirabeau's] absence Talleyrand was making love to his [Mirabeau's] mistress may have been responsible for the vigour of this denunciation, and, in spite of it, the two men became again, almost immediately, the firmest of friends."

Cooper believes, however, that the Directory was less revolutionary than its press releases. He writes: "The Directory, which ruled France for four years, from November, 1795, to November, 1799, had only one principle—to protect in their existing situation the large number of people who had made substantial profits out of the Revolution." He goes on: "The outward forms of the Revolution were still observed, the new calendar and the new jargon. Toy dogs were trained to growl at the name of an aristocrat, every tenth day was *décadi* and the excuse for a gala, at which Monsieur and Madame addressed one another with equal politeness as Citizen and Citizeness."

Although he had a long working relationship with the emperor, Talleyrand did remark once, after Napoleon had delivered a tirade (it appears in Cooper): "What a pity that such a great man should be so ill-bred." Apparently among the bon mots that ended his relationship with the emperor was his remark that "if a gentleman commits follies, if he keeps mistresses, if he treats his wife badly, even if he is guilty of serious injustices towards his friends, he will be blamed, no doubt, but if he is rich, powerful, and intelligent, society will still treat him with indulgence. But if that man cheats at cards he will be immediately banished from decent society and never forgiven." In turn, Napoleon never forgave Talleyrand, who, ever the diplomat, went to work for his successor.

As we strolled through the back gardens, the tour guide referred to Talleyrand's onetime lover Madame Germaine de Staël, the daughter of his colleague and rival, Jacques Necker. Talleyrand and Madame de Staël were present when Napoleon had just taken power, and a coming-out party for him was given at Hotel Matignon. While she was in imperial favor, Madame de Staël even put in a word for Talleyrand to become foreign minister.

Following her own falling out with Napoleon (who asked, "What does that woman want?"), Madame de Staël moved her famous literary and political salon to Coppet, on the shores of Lake Geneva in Switzerland. From there she kept up her tumultuous relationship with Talleyrand. Cooper writes: "No man could rise to prominence except against the background of a *salon*, and over every *salon* a woman ruled."

Later, after the couple had broken up, she included an unflattering portrait of a Talleyrand-like character in one of her novels. The former lover shot back: "I see in her new novel that Madame de Staël has disguised both of us as women."

Flaubert Wields His Pen as if it Were a Scalpel

Rouen

BEFORE LEAVING PARIS FOR ORLÉANS, I decided to make a side trip to Rouen, to see the house where the writer Gustave Flaubert was born. In researching his writing life, which overlapped with the Second Empire (1852–70), I discovered that the house in Croisset where he spent most of his life had been torn down,[3] but that his birthplace in Rouen, where his father was a famous doctor and surgeon, was a museum that oddly combined literature and medicine. Was it because, as many of his biographers have pointed out, Flaubert wielded his pen as if it were a scalpel?

The train departed Gare Saint-Lazare in late morning. I hadn't bothered to pick an exact train, so when I showed up and discovered I had an hour's wait, I bought my ticket and rode my bike down to the Seine, which the local train would later follow for about an hour out of the city. I had never taken a train along its banks, and I was surprised that

---

3: Flaubert described it to his niece: "The moon is coming through the tulip tree; the boats cast dark shadows on the drowsy Seine, the trees are reflected on the water, the rhythmical sound of oars breaks the silence; it is utterly exquisite."

they were lined more with industrial plants and warehouses than Impressionist pathways and small boats tacking in the breeze. Occasionally through the train window I would catch glimpses of the river, and always I thought of the Mississippi near St. Louis rather than Monet's gardens.

Although Flaubert is associated with the city—he called *A Sentimental Education* his Paris novel—he was a product of the provincial life and wrote most of his novels in a manor house overlooking the Seine, very much the kind of bourgeois gentleman that he hoped to satirize in his writing. He was born, however, in a detached city house in Rouen that is on the grounds of the Hotel de Ville (off Avenue Gustave Flaubert, naturally). I bought a ticket to wander through the family apartment, which is divided between plastic cadavers and portraits of women suspected to have been the models for Madame Emma Bovary. I preferred the surgeries dealing with adultery over those handling circulatory problems, although it was clear to me that all the cabinets, in one form or another, were exposing the human heart.

I would like to report that I came to the Musée Flaubert et d'Histoire de la Médecine as an expert on his life, but the reality is that when I ascended his staircase—lined with busts and portraits of his illustrious forebears ("This is your father's house and you are a Flaubert")—my familiarity with Flaubert's writing was limited to a reading of *Madame Bovary* in my thirties and several more recent attempts to get past page 124 of *A Sentimental Education*. I didn't know anything about Flaubert as a person, which is why when I was back home I tracked down *Flaubert: A Life* by Geoffrey Wall, who filled me in on the genius who either imagined or described the romantic temptations of a married woman living in a Normandy village called Yonville-l'Abbaye.

So thin are the lines in the literature of French realism between an author's imagination and experiences that, since the publication of *Madame Bovary* in 1857, a cottage industry has flourished trying to out the real Madame Bovary among a list of local candidates, all of whom, apparently, were bored with their husbands and not above a dalliance with the equivalent of Rodolphe Boulanger (no relation to the general). Little did Emma know that when she longed to escape Yonville-l'Abbaye for the bright lights of the city, she was also doing her best to get out of a tourist trap, which now commemorates her passions with restaurants, hotels, and walking tour plaques, just so it's clear to modern readers that all Flaubert did in his novel was write up a local affair, as if it were a cover story for *Vanity Fair*.

In the museum, I happily joined this local parlor game and inspected all sorts of postcards, prints, paintings, and statues (many from the nearby village of Ry), which try to pinpoint Emma's actual townhouse and Rodolphe's *garçonniere*, now spruced up into the Château de la Huchette. Looking at some of the cabinets in the museum, I could almost hear some neighbors whispering: "I'm pretty sure she was that tramp, Madame. . ." Elsewhere, on a door paneling, there was a list of the contents of Flaubert's wine cellar—containing vintages from Bordeaux, Volnay, Sauternes, Chambertin, Beaune, Graves, and Champagne—and painted on the walls were quotations from his books ("I love nothing more than theater").

The biographical Flaubert—at least that of Wall—is less interesting than the author of *Madame Bovary*, who comes across as enlightened, sympathetic, cosmopolitan, engaged, and observant, the kind of person you would love to have at a dinner party. In reality, Flaubert strikes me as someone who was often morose, moody, pedantic, reclusive, and given to pronouncements. Even his great friend the female writer George Sand said of him: "He never wants to do anything but talk about literature." She also noted: "He doesn't like noise, but he doesn't mind the din he makes himself." Nevertheless, Sand was one of the few friends whom Flaubert didn't drive away from his narrow circle. Many others were sent packing, including Louise Pradier, one of the few loves in his life. Wall concludes: "Making trouble, like Byron, like Rabelais, had long been a vital part of Flaubert's artistic ambition." Much of this rebellion, when not directed at his austere parents, was aimed at the Second Empire.

Coming of age in Rouen, Flaubert suffered from his parents' high expectations for their son Gustave. His father was a distinguished surgeon, and his mother imagined him a country squire, perhaps the reason they pushed him to attend law school. In a sentence that would draw the attention of Freudian psychologists, Flaubert confessed: "The law leaves me in a state of moral castration." Wall writes of his legal studies: "A dismal mixture of grandiosity, ambition, fury, grief, and self-hatred, one dark night it all exploded in his head."

Flaubert might have enjoyed his travels—treks across France in the style of Robert Louis Stevenson and excursions on the Nile—had he not been so self-absorbed. His traveling companion Maxime du Camp said: "Flaubert would have travelled on a divan, lying down, without moving, watching the landscapes, the ruins and the cities passing in front of his eyes like the canvas unrolling in a panorama-machine."

Nevertheless, on the Nile he came up with the name Emma Bovary. He filled notebooks with observations across the Mediterranean and beyond ("Jerusalem strikes me as a fortified charnel-house; old religions are silently rotting away there, you tread on turds and all you can see is ruins: it's immensely sad"). No matter where he was, it could be argued, his mind remained in Rouen.

Despite his reputation as the poet laureate of bored housewives—*Madame Bovary* is the story of doomed, extramarital passions in provincial France—Flaubert never married and had a tempestuous relationship with his mother, perhaps the reason he found sexual solace mainly with prostitutes. (Wall: "Looking for the Mother was already the great theme of Flaubert's erotic quest.") He was intimately acquainted with many venereal diseases, to the point of including in his *Dictionary of Received Wisdom* a definition for syphilis ("Everyone, more or less, is affected by it") and the cure ("Mercury—Finishes off the patient along with the disease)." With such a background, how did he manage to write one of the masterpieces of nineteenth-century literature, especially on a subject (marriage) about which he had no firsthand knowledge?

One of Flaubert's redeeming gifts as a writer was that he read well and widely and, when his nerves would allow it, was a great listener. Wall writes: "He loved listening to women. . . . His habitual simulations of the feminine, whatever else they might signify, underlie the wonderful psychological intimacies of *Madame Bovary*." Despite his personal awkwardness, literature allowed Flaubert to enter cloistered worlds that without his writing he might never have seen. He confesses (as is quoted in Wall): "It is a delectable thing, writing, not having to be yourself, being able to circulate in amongst the whole creation that you are describing. . . . For me a book has always only been a way of living in some particular milieu. That is what explains my hesitations, my anguish and my slowness."

Flaubert equated his books with his travels—"A novel, whatever its subject, is like a long journey; I hesitate and my heart aches before I set off." He also said: "But we don't choose our subjects, we submit to them." Not for a minute did he pattern Emma Bovary after a woman in Ry or even his lover Louise Pradier ("the very type of womanhood with all its instincts, an orchestra of female sentiment"), for the same reason that he despised seeing illustrations in his published books. "They only make you think of one woman," he said, "but a woman in writing makes the reader dream of a thousand women." He described his hopes for the novel that became *Madame Bovary*: "I will have known your sufferings, poor obscure souls, damp from your stifled sorrows, like your provincial back-yards, where the moss grows on the walls."

Given that Flaubert's writing life largely overlapped with Napoleon III's Second Empire, to what extent can his novels be read as political protests? To be sure, the government reaction to Emma Bovary's lusts was to condemn and vilify Flaubert as a corrupter of public morals. The novel was what in French is called a *succès de scandale* (a scandalous success), and the charges brought against Flaubert were for "offending public morality, religion and decency." He wrote (it appears in Wall): "I have been attacked by the government, by the priests and by the newspapers." He was acquitted, although the trial only sharpened his pencil against the excesses of Napoleon III and the Second Empire.

In Flaubert's case, Wall writes: "Henceforth, it was Art against Empire." He had declared an artistic war on his tormentors. Flaubert wrote: "We are heading for a new Babylon. Why not? The Individual has been so thoroughly disparaged by Democracy that he will submit to being utterly obliterated, just as happened under the great theocratic tyrannies." He went on: "For it was all a fake: fake army, fake politics, fake literature, fake credit and even fake whores. To have told the truth would have been an act of immorality." After it was swept away at Sedan, he reflected: "France was like a sick room. Everyone spoke in a whisper," although in his *Dictionary* he writes, again with Freudian overtones: "They cannot find our souls with their scalpels."

Joan of Arc's Hometown
Orléans and the Loire

I TOOK A TWO-HOUR NIGHT TRAIN TO ORLÉANS, departing Paris from Gare Austerlitz. (After the battle of the same name, Talleyrand wrote to Napoleon I: "The Austrian monarchy is a combination of ill-assorted states, differing from one another in language, manners, religion, and constitution, and having only one thing in common—the identity of their ruler.") The station, while once glorious, looked as though it was renovated in the 1960s, when mediocre urban planners grafted on to the nineteenth-century railroad palace an office building, waiting rooms, and sandwich shops, making it look as though Amtrak were running the SNCF.

The train had no compartment for bikes, so I had to dismount the front wheel and wedge the bike frame into a luggage rack. On arrival at 11 p.m., Orléans was magical, with soft spotlights bathing the exterior of its cathedral and royal palaces. Because I wasn't tired, I rode through the historic quarter before tracking down a hotel. The kindly manager let me leave my bike in the lobby. The next morning he served me the most sumptuous breakfast of the trip, gave me a bike map of the Loire Valley, and encouraged me to wrap up some sandwiches from the buffet for the road.

This was my first visit to Orléans, and I loved its gran-deur. On the bike I followed the markers of a walking tour so that I could see the house where Joan of Arc (the Maid of Orléans) was said to have lived. The museum was closed, but the house had the look of something built in the early twentieth century, unless Joan was also a revolutionary in her architectural habits and put up a beamed row house in 1429 (and later added the satellite dish and what look like Tudor trimmings).

From my books and maps, I knew that the last battles of the Franco-Prussian war took place around Orléans. After Sedan, the theater of operations in the Franco-Prussian war shifted to sieges around Paris and Orléans, where the French, through a *levée en masse*, raised a new ragtag army of five hundred thousand men to take on the invading Germans. Although it wasn't much of a fighting force, the militia army did change the face of battle from the engagements of pro-fessional armies into more of a guerrilla campaign, which favored the French. They won a handful of victories, nota-bly at Coulmiers, giving heart to the new government, which by then had shifted to Tours. (Dramatically, and no doubt to the great pleasure of Jules Verne, Prime Minister Gambetta escaped from besieged Paris in a balloon.)

Even when the Germans took Orléans, the fighting raged on in the countryside, forcing the Germans to divert men and material to protect their rear as they were moving in to besiege Paris. In the end, the siege of Paris and the subse-quent bombardment of the city ended the war, although what France lost at Metz and Sedan it partly recovered around Orléans, notably a glimmer of self-respect for its armies. While at the same time, not all German politicians and commanders approved of the general staff's and Bismarck's decisions to march troops so deep into France. It was one thing to take Sedan and Metz, both frontier cities. From Metz to Orléans was a distance of two hundred miles on roads that at best were primitive.

Because I could not do justice in a few days to the campaign that was fought between Orléans and Paris, I decided, instead of going to Coulmiers, to bike along the river Loire toward Blois. I had often read that the Loire was ideal for bike riding, with paths along the river and past glorious châteaux, and I would end up in Tours, another city that I did not know. The manager's cycling guide to the Loire showed a path running serenely along the riverbanks and through medieval towns, although when I set off I discovered that the famous cycling route is a work in progress.

In some stretches, the path was as presented in the brochure—a segregated cycle lane marked with signs about points of interests and picnic tables near the water. When some town didn't care much for the idea or the expense, the path was handled with a few signs or arrows. Repeatedly, during the long day, I would find myself trying to figure out where I had made a wrong turn and how I had ended up off the prescribed way. Medieval towns such as Beaugency, where I stopped for coffee and to browse in the shops, were lovely, but down the river, around Saint-Laurent Nouan, I got lost and ended up in front of a nuclear power station, which somehow is omitted from the glossy cycle-path brochure.

The ride to Blois took about three hours. There I succumbed to the pleasures of tourism and had lunch at an outdoor restaurant looking up at the Royal Château de Blois, famous as the place where Catherine de Medici (sent from

Florence to marry Henri, the second son of King François I) is said to have stashed her poisons.

As queen mother and regent for several of her sons, Catherine presided over a reign of terror from 1559 to 1589—carrying out the 1572 St. Bartholomew's Day massacre in Paris by the Catholics against the Protestant Huguenots, poisoning her rivals (apparently with treated gloves), and even abusing her children (she executed her daughter Margaret's lover and disowned the child).

On the positive side, Catherine held the French monarchy together with her iron fists and the dynastic marriages of her children. She even tried to reconcile the Huguenots with the Catholic monarchy. No wonder that in her fictional memoirs she is quoted as saying: "Love is a treacherous emotion. You will fare better without it. We Medici always have."

Graham Robb Discovers France
South from Tours

FROM THE LOIRE VALLEY I decided to head to Biarritz, on the southwest coast of France, just north of the Spanish border. But I was in no rush to get there on a direct TGV express from Tours and chose instead to meander on local trains through central France. I discovered these regional trains when I was searching the schedules for rail service that would easily accommodate my bicycle. Not all TGVs have bike compartments, and space in them is limited.

These trains were part of the TER network (*Transport express régional*) and stopped everywhere, in the style of American milk trains. Unlike those on the cramped TGVs, the seats were ample and many came with a small desk, under which there was power for my computer. The large windows provided plenty of light to read, and the trains cut through parts of France that I had never seen.

The landscape—at once rich and desolate—led me a book entitled *The Discovery of France: Historical Geography from the Revolution to the First World War*. The author is Graham Robb, and he is a scholar of French history and literature, according to the book jacket, having previously written biographies of Balzac, Hugo, and Rimbaud. The used copy I bought once belonged to the Cliffside Park Free Public

Library, on the Palisades in New Jersey. According to the card in the back, no one there ever checked out the book, which is a shame, as Robb has put together a compendium about France that surprises on every page and illuminated my slow train rides across *la France profonde* (deep France).

Robb's conclusion is that the country we call France was, until about two hundred years ago, as geographically uncharted as the American West and as fractured in its thought, speech, and habits as parts of the Balkans or Russia. "At the time of the French Revolution," he writes, "almost four-fifths of the population was rural. . . . Before the mid-nineteenth century, few people had seen a map of France and few had heard of Charlemagne and Joan of Arc. . . . They belonged to a town, a suburb, a village or a family, not a nation or a province." He quotes from a book published in 1837: "Each valley is still a little world which differs from the neighboring world as Mercury does from Uranus. Each village is a clan, a kind of state with its own form of patriotism." The goal of most villages was to shut themselves off from the outside world. At late as 1835, a "witch" was burned in Beaumont-en-Cambrésis.

Nor was French the spoken language of France. "News of important events and government decrees," Robb describes, "left the capital on the broad river of French only to run aground in the muddy creeks of patois." In the 1850s only about 10 percent of the population spoke French. Languages confronted on the way from Lyon to Bordeaux would have been Savoyard, Lyonnais, Auvergnat, Limousin, and finally Girondin. In the twentieth century, he writes, "There are several reports of Breton soldiers being shot by their comrades in the First World War because they were mistaken for

Germans or because they failed to obey incomprehensible orders." Charles de Gaulle asked famously: "How can one be expected to govern a country that has two hundred and forty-six different kinds of cheese?"

Nor can it be said that religion bound together such a rural, fragmented society. Robb explains: "The Virgin Mary was always more important than God. Like his son, God offered neither redemption nor forgiveness. He had been known to destroy towns and to cause road accidents just to make his point. . . . The saints performed miraculous cures, but they had to be cajoled and bullied like lazy public servants."

Worshippers preferred the lives of the saints to those of the Creator, as Robb attests: "Even in Brittany, which was supposed to be a bastion of Catholicism, the Church was important in the same way that a shopping mall is important to shoppers: the customers were not especially interested in the creator and owner of the mall; they came to see the saints, who sold their wares in little chapels around the nave."

The population put much store in miracles, however, given that "a ten-minute hailstorm could wipe out the work of a generation, demolishing roofs, stripping trees, flattening crops, and covering the ground with a carpet of twigs, leaves, and small dead birds." In Auvergne, a popular expression was: "If only God was a decent man."

Travel in the nineteenth and early twentieth centuries across France was a nightmare—something to consider when I was weighing how German troops fared marching from Sedan to Orléans. "Most French roads," Robb writes, "were designed by architects rather than road engineers; many bridges were beautiful works of art until they collapsed in the river." He explains that the "French word *route*, which means both 'route' and 'road', preserves the ambiguity." Nor was my experience in the Loire much different from that of early tourists. Robb writes: "The Loire, which was supposed to be the cradle of French civilization, disappointed many travelers with its mudflats, its wispy poplars, and its monotonous, misty banks."

Rather than open up France to the outside, the coming of the railways erased many towns and villages that had previously been on well-trod routes. "Soon," Robb says, "the railways would empty the roads and ruin the roadside inns. They would close off large parts of the country whilst giving passengers the illusion that France was now open to discovery. . . . No sooner did poets and art lovers learn of the existence of this magical land than they found it in ruins." He quotes one traveler from that era: "We shall see much, but learn little."

Changing Trains with Balzac
Angoulême to Bordeaux

I HAD THE THOUGHT OF A STOP in Poitiers long enough to see the battlefield there (in his *Chronicles* Jean Froissart writes: "It began in the early morning and was finished by mid-afternoon, although many of the English did not return from the pursuit until late evening. . . . There died that day, it was said, the finest flower of French chivalry, whereby the realm of France was sorely weakened and fell into great misery and affliction. . ."), but when I rolled out of the train station on my bicycle, I headed into a downpour, which dampened my enthusiasm for more research into the Hundred Years War.

Further south, I did manage to stop in Angoulême, an attractive city by a river with a large Romanesque church that during the Revolution would have been called a "temple of reason." The city hall is built into a castle, in case those coming to renew their dog licenses break out a few catapults.

Angoulême is where Balzac sets the scene for *Lost Illusions*, the story of Lucien de Rubempré's social and professional climb from the provinces and poetry to Paris and journalism. Of Lucien's ambitions, Balzac writes: "He thought of nothing but his one desire, the patent of nobility; for he saw clearly that for him such a restoration meant a wealthy marriage, and, the title once secured, chance and his good looks would do the rest."

I had downloaded various Balzac novels onto my Kindle during one of my train rides, and he never failed to delight and inform me on the fleeting landscape outside my window. For example, he says of the press: "A newspaper is not supposed to enlighten its readers, but to supply them with congenial opinions." On lawyers he writes: "These weighty matters of the law completely fill the country attorney's mind; he has a bill of costs always before his eyes, whereas his brother of Paris thinks of nothing but his fees."

I agreed with Balzac's view on government. He writes: "Learn that the first principle of government is this—never to have been in the wrong, and that the instinct of power and the sense of dignity is even stronger in women than in governments." On Lucien's fall from society's grace, he writes: "The Medicis, Richelieu, and Napoleon started from precisely your standpoint; but they, my child, considered that their prospects were worth ingratitude, treachery, and the most glaring inconsistencies." I am sorry that Balzac died in 1851, the year before Napoleon III came to power. Theirs would have been a match made in the literary heavens. Nevertheless, much of what he wrote about France came true in the Second Empire.

Earlier in my travels, while in Paris, I had gone to the house where Balzac wrote many of his novels between midnight and 6 a.m. There I saw the small coffeepot, warmed with a candle, that fueled so much of his fiction. ("This coffee falls into your stomach, and straightway there is a general commotion. Ideas begin to move like the battalions of the Grand Army on the battlefield, and the battle takes place.")

The museum has some of his galley proofs, on which he made extensive changes, testament to his passion for rewriting and correction before the era of cut-and-paste function keys. In another room are small porcelain figurines of nearly all the characters in *La Comédie humaine*, some twenty volumes that my father had on our shelves when I was growing up. I found the statuesque Lucien de Rubempré very much the man about town. As Balzac writes: "One cannot act the lover's part in rags."

After Angoulême, I biked the contours of the Bordeaux vineyards and tasted some of their magnificent wines. The distance from Médoc to Saint-Émilion is some sixty miles (not all of it is covered with vineyards), so I used a combination of commuter trains and my bike to explore the appellations of Pauillac, Saint-Julien, Margaux, and Pomerol, each of which came with their special charms. The left bank of the Gironde River has such famous châteaux as those of Lafite Rothschild and Mouton Rothschild, which appear as baronial manor houses looming above the vineyards, while the estates on the right bank of the river are, comparatively speaking, more modest. Around Petrus (in Pomerol) all I could find were a few outbuildings, although what looked like a marble palace was under construction. And I was surprised to find that the only wine village with any charm was Saint-Émilion, which has restaurants and wine cellars squeezed between the ramparts of the walled town. By contrast, the towns of Margaux and Pauillac, sainted as they might be in the wine world, are little more than agricultural way stations, places where it is a struggle to buy a sandwich or coffee. At least Bordeaux is at the center of the wine country, and it's a delight of cobblestoned streets, elegant bookstores, and a sweeping esplanade along the riverbank.

Finding a connection in Bordeaux to the Franco-Prussian war proved a harder hill to climb, although I discovered online an academic article that concluded that French wine exports to Germany increased after the 1870 war. The paper states: "Inversely, one could argue that the Germans enjoyed an extra utility from consuming goods representing the French culture, pushing further the humiliation of the defeat on France." When I read that, I knew I had gone too far. And when I laughed out loud about my strange Franco-Prussian obsession, I knew that the worst aspects of grief were passing.

A Second Empire Thrift Shop
Biarritz

FROM BORDEAUX I TOOK THE TRAIN to Biarritz, where
Napoleon III built a seaside palace in honor of his wife,
Empress Eugenie, and where there is now a Second Empire
museum.

The beach resort is two hours on the train south of Bordeaux, but unfortunately I did not get there until late autumn,
when it was very much out of season. Surfers in wet suits
were still catching the waves that roll into the town's sheltered bay, but I walked along the sea under threatening winter clouds and huddled in the Eugenie Palace Hotel to drink
coffee, not summer wines.

Biarritz is more like Monte Carlo or St. Tropez—
small cities that have grown up around famous seaside
hotels—than it is like East Hampton or Santorini. Set
around a half-moon beach, backed with high-rise apartments, it looks as though a number of modern cruise ships
have run aground on the rocks and been converted to con-
dos. The city center of Biarritz has a graceful square, and
not far from the downtown is the famous Golf du Phare—
one of the first golf courses on the continent. The beach
is bracketed with rocky promontories, and when a gale is
blowing in from the treacherous Bay of Biscay it throws

spray over the breakwaters, giving the resort some of its fleeting magic.

Not many tourists come to Biarritz in November, and even fewer were waiting at 10 a.m. for the Biarritz Historical Museum to open. I bought a ticket from the unpleasant clerk, who lectured me about not taking any pictures. At a glance, the museum has the air of a large Second Empire thrift shop, where, perhaps, the Napoleons donated their clothes and old furniture after abdicating in September 1870.

The museum tells the story of Biarritz as it evolved from a Basque whaling village to a playground for nineteenth-century royalty. Empress Eugenie spent summers here as a girl, and Napoleon III had a palace built on the beach to please her, so that she would have the choice of about one hundred rooms in which to change into her bathing costume. The imperial couple's presence on the beach pioneered the pastime of swimming, then unknown in France, and the French embraced it, as a modified way of taking the waters.

In time, Biarritz became a summer watering hole of royalty. In many museum cabinets I saw displays devoted to the exiled Queen of Serbia, the Grand Duke of Russia (who adopted a brave dog that earlier saved some sailors), and Queen Victoria (not dressed for swimming), all of whom took suites overlooking the beach sands that are still groomed daily.

In 1865 Biarritz was also where Bismarck came to take the measure of Napoleon III before deciding whether to move toward showdowns with Austria and, afterward, France. Guedalla writes in *The Second Empire*:

Late in 1865, when the Court was at Biarritz, he [Bismarck] came himself to consult the dull eyes of the oracle. The big, bald man drove up to the Villa Eugénie; and as the great Biscayan rollers broke along the coast, he talked interminably to the Emperor. There were no promises; but as their talk trailed slowly across the map, Bismarck could see that Venice still haunted *il muto Imperator*, that he would abet a war in which Venice might be won for Italy. *Le spectre de Venise erre dans les salles des Tuileries.* It had beckoned once; and Napoleon sent Maximilian to Mexico. It beckoned again; he stared and sent the Prussians to Sadowa [a famous defeat to the Germans].

While Bismarck was staring down the French emperor, and deciding he was ripe for a picking, he would have thought, too, about the magical summer of 1862 when he fell hopelessly in love with a Russian princess, Kathy Orlov, despite having a wife and family back in Prussia. (Kathy had a husband in Biarritz.)

Whether their romance in Biarritz was consummated or not, Bismarck spent his free time courting the princess, whom he would never see again, despite his obvious affections and their long correspondence. Fortunately for him, he was married to an understanding woman, Johanna von Puttkamer, who was as pleased as her husband with the emotional liaison, writing (it appears Crankshaw's biography of Bismarck):

> Were I at all inclined to jealousy and envy I should be tyrannized to the depths now by these passions. But my soul has no room for them and I rejoice quite enormously that my beloved husband has found this

charming woman. But for her he would never have found peace for long in one place or become so well as he boasts of being in every letter.

Not only would Bismarck find love in Biarritz, but he would also find empire, as five summers after his last visit to that shore he would be accepting Napoleon III's sword in Donchery and sending him packing to his games of whist in Germany.

Biarritz is the kind of place where you can imagine Noel Coward, after a long night in the casino, sleeping late, although one novel of the Second Empire contains the line "I generally get up in the morning." In the museum there are many pictures of stars from the period between the world wars, arriving at swank hotels in convertible sports cars. The Nazis put a temporary end to the fun, converting the harbor into one of the linchpins of their Atlantic Wall.

Immediately after World War II, the Americans equally failed to appreciate the charms of the seaside resort, using it to set up a self-improvement university for GIs still in France. From the photographs, they look as though they were majoring in dalliances, although the museum also has some pictures of the somber commanding general, answering correspondence at his desk. Nevertheless, the heyday of Biarritz was when it served as the summer capital of the Second Empire (1852–1870). The real story of that imperial masquerade—to use the title of S. C. Burchell's account of the period—will never get into the museum cabinets.

Bonapartism Goes on Vacation
Biarritz

MOVING ABOUT, I read often about the reign of Napoleon III and his empress Eugenie. Besides Burchell, Philip Guedalla has his history, *The Second Empire*, and other historians of the Franco-Prussian War include narratives about how a down-and-out nephew of Napoleon Bonaparte, with few qualifications more than a role as an extra in a Gilbert and Sullivan musical, came to rule France for almost twenty years and then led it to military disaster at Sedan.

Nothing quite matches Louis Napoleon's initial foray into power politics. Guedalla sets the opulent stage, describing how in 1836:

> Bonapartism . . . was the barren enthusiasm for the memory of a dead man. . . . Napoleon had been exiled on a rock in the Atlantic: his nephew (it was typical of the more crowded atmosphere of a later age) was exiled to New York. . . . This circle, from which he received a good deal of hospitality, found him well-mannered but somewhat silent, with an odd tendency to discuss his destiny and his future reign on the throne of France.

The nephew would say, "My power is an immortal name," although Théophile Gautier said "he looks like a ringmaster who has been sacked for getting drunk." As quoted by Burchell, Karl Marx was equally wary, calling the followers of Louis Napoleon "a collection of 'vagabonds, disbanded soldiers, discharged prisoners, fugitives from the galleys, sharpers, jugglers, professional beggars, pickpockets, conjurers, gamesters, pimps, brothel-keepers' and so forth." Graham Robb picks up the rise-to-power story in *The Discovery of France*:

> In August 1840, Napoleon's nephew also made himself a laughing-stock by chartering a pleasure boat in London and sailing to Boulogne-sur-Mer with sixty men and a caged vulture masquerading as an imperial eagle. . . . Yet two years after escaping from prison disguised as a labourer with a plank of wood to hide his face, Louis-Napoleon was elected President of France.

The year 1848 was a bad one for European monarchies, although the French split their opposition ticket when they elected a royal pretender, Louis Napoleon, to the presidency. Four years later he decided that electoral politics was a tawdry occupation for a Bonaparte (his father was Napoleon's brother and his mother the daughter of Josephine, so he had a double case of the family disease), and in 1852 he successfully staged a coup d'état and proclaimed the Second Empire.

One reason why he chose to dismiss the Assembly was its refusal to appropriate money and manpower for what he called "a war of sentiment," something easier to fund with an empire. As quoted by Guedalla, the British ambassador to Paris said: "The Emperor's mind seems as full of schemes as a warren is full of rabbits." A year later France eagerly signed up for the Crimean War, and splendid little wars were often featured in Napoleon III's lavish stage productions.

The Second Empire was a hit in Paris. During this time Baron Haussmann gave Paris a makeover, and Guedalla notes: "The broad, new streets which drove through the town were beautifully accessible to light, air, and infantry." Gaiety returned to the palaces. "It began to seem that the Goncourts were right," Burchell explains, "when they said that only four things mattered at the Tuileries: youth, beauty, diamonds— and a dress."

Even the devoted family man, Napoleon III, was swept up in the predominating spirit of a masked ball, and it was his prerogative to cut in whenever he chose. Burchell explains the protocol for the dance floor:

> As a rule, the imperial approach was less subtle. The emperor would simply go up to a lady who had caught his fancy, twist the points of his mustache and murmur in her ear: Until tonight.

Of an early year in Napoleon III's reign passed, Graham Brooks writes in his *Great Lives* biography:

> So the year passed. Stag-hunting at Compiegne; whispering to the voluptuous [Comtesse de] Castiglione in the moonlit gardens of the Tuileries; slinking through the postern to snatch an evening with Miss Howard; sauntering through the wooded glades round Fontainebleau; playing in turn the libertine and proud husband, the autocrat and genie of the lamp, with kings for pawns, a nation's happiness at stake, and plaudits ringing in his ears – to the phantom Caesar, life seemed all gossamer in 1856.

Not everyone, however, was giving the emperor rave reviews that he gave himself. "It's all very beautiful today," said the poet Alfred de Musset, which appears in Burchell. "Yes, for the moment very beautiful. But I wouldn't give you two sous for the last act."

While the emperor could have his way with giggling coquettes, he was less seductive in foreign affairs, which did not have the habit of bowing before his name. In 1864 he installed an Austrian prince, Maximilian, on the vacant throne of Mexico, hoping to revive the empire overseas. The United States was distracted with its Civil War and had put the Monroe Doctrine on hold, but afterward Union troops along the Mexican border compelled Napoleon to withdraw Marshal Bazaine's troops. "The Mexican expedition was, in its first phase, a bondholder's war," Guedalla writes, adding that "the Prince never recovered from the hallucination that he understood the United States; and it was not until thirty years later, when he had sent Maximilian to Mexico, that he learnt his error."

In 1867 the Mexicans dispatched Maximilian with a firing squad, prompting Guedalla to observe that "to Napoleon the sudden fall of an Empire in Mexico must have come with the vague menace of lightning below the horizon." Burchell goes further: "The death of Maximilian, occurring thousands of miles from France, marked a beginning to the end of the Second Empire—in spite of all the prosperity and splendor and aggressive materialism in the exposition year. Something was desperately wrong, and the news from Mexico contained a part of the answer."

Nor did Napoleon ever take the correct measure of Bismarck, despite their long talks on the beach in Biarritz.

Brooks writes:

> Certain it is that he was not the man of the Empire's
> early days. If proof were needed, it lies in the facility with
> which Bismarck duped him at the Biarritz interview in
> 1865, when the Iron Chancellor extracted a promise of
> France's neutrality during the coming hostilities against
> Austria, in return for an illusory promise of Luxembourg.

The German chancellor was looking for a showdown with Austria, as a way to unite northern and southern Germany under Prussian leadership. The emperor could have been a deterrent if he had made a strong stand alongside the Austrians. Instead of coming to Vienna's defense, he merely wished for an Austrian victory at Sadowa in 1866 and, like the rest of Europe, expressed astonishment when the Prussians easily crushed the Austrians. The emperor never seemed to grasp the truism of the time: "Prussia is not a country which has an army. Prussia is an army which has a country."

When contemplating the result, Napoleon III would have done well to listen to the words of the French politician Adolphe Thiers, who said: "It is we who were beaten at Sadowa." Instead, he came late to the Austrian funeral, yet still asked Bismarck for part of the inheritance. (He hoped for some slices of Italy.) Guedalla writes: "Since Bismarck was disinclined to be given prizes which he had already taken, the Emperor was left making dignified gestures to an empty class-room." Bismarck dismissed Napoleon's demands as *"la note de l'aubergiste"* ("the innkeeper's bill") and started making his plans for Sedan.

Even then, the empire might have averted disaster if the Austrians had fought on the side of the French in 1870. In the run-up to war, Burchell writes, "the Emperor had gone to Salzburg in search of an ally; he had found only a neutral." When the fighting began, Austria wanted no part of another war with Prussia, especially after the early battles near Metz went so poorly for the French. By that point Napoleon was on his own—grimacing from his kidney stone, unable to figure out the Prussian encirclement, and riding with Marshal Mac-Mahon toward Sedan.

Despite the ban, I did take two pictures at the Biarritz Historical Museum. For an hour I was the only one there, and the woman at the desk who had warned me against it was shouting into her cellphone. I took one picture of Napoleon standing for a portrait. He is wearing black riding boots, white breeches, and a red sash across his chest. His expression matches a description given him by another American at the 1867 Paris Exposition: "A long-bodied, short-legged man, fiercely mustached, old, wrinkled, with eyes half closed, and *such* a deep, crafty, scheming expression about them!" The poet Baudelaire wrote: "Who among us is not a duplex man?" although in the case of Napoleon III, I wonder if the elevator was out of order.

The other picture I took was of a portrait of Empress Eugenie. It was displayed on a painter's easel in front of several (yes, Second Empire) chairs that were scattered about, as though a game of whist had ended late. Unlike other paintings of her in the museum, she is not seated in a gazebo looking out to sea, but wearing a tiara and dressed in a gown, perhaps heading to a ball in her waterfront palace. Her expression is that of someone going through the official motions but who would rather be outside at the beach, collecting seashells. Was it about such scenes that

Baudelaire wrote the words that Edna St. Vincent Millay later translated?

And a grey sky was drizzling down
Upon this sad, lethargic world.

Their "lethargic" world ended in the artillery shells that destroyed the French lines around Sedan. Nevertheless, Burchell sees other reasons for the fall and quotes from a novel set during Eugenie's reign:

It was not immorality which destroyed the Second Empire nor unsound financial practices nor misplaced concepts of glory—nor even the Prussians. The empire fell through its denial of reality—a denial nourished by middle-class hypocrisy and an insolent display of luxury.

After Sedan, Eugenie tried to govern for a while in her husband's absence, but soon she was forced to flee to exile in England, where she lived like other royal exiles would in Biarritz. Leaving the Tuileries Palace disguised as a maid, she uttered her most famous words: "In no country in the world is the step between the sublime and the ridiculous so short as in this." Later a Parisian remarked of the vanished era: "You can still have a good time, but it's not the same thing."

Otto von Bismarck Becomes an Innkeeper
Friedrichsruh, Germany

IN BIARRITZ, I GOT THE IDEA to end this story not in France at all, but in Germany, at the Bismarck villa and museum. Until I looked it up online, however, I didn't know where it was located. I found several Bismarck houses around Germany, as befits his standing as the Iron Chancellor and hero of German unification. Further scrolling around websites told me that the main research center, the Bismarck Museum, and his gravesite are located in Friedrichsruh, a suburb of Hamburg. French rail passes are not valid in Germany—the conditions of Versailles were not that harsh—but I had no trouble booking an overnight sleeper from Basel to Hamburg and connecting on a commuter train to Friedrichsruh, which appears to have little more than its Bismarck shrines.

Arriving early, I spent the half hour before the museum opened walking under the mainline train tracks to the chapel where lie the tombs of Bismarck and his forgiving wife, Johanna. A somber affair, the chapel is a cross between a family crypt and a national monument, and the tombs are the size of marble tool sheds. Even the inscription on his tomb—"A true German servant of Emperor William I"—has Bismarck speaking his mind. It was a gloomy November morning, with cold freezing mist and scattered wet leaves on the ground, and I was sorry that nowhere in town was anyone selling coffee.

Walking back to the museum, I discovered that the Bismarck Foundation had its offices in the train station of Friedrichsruh. A secretary was on duty, and she was excited that someone had come from Switzerland, in November, to see the exhibits. I explained to her that I had written ahead, hoping to see the museum's director, but that he had written back to say that he would be away that day.

No, she said, he was upstairs. In that German way, she left her desk and went upstairs to fetch him. What had him so busy on a misty Thursday in November, in such a sleepy corner of Germany, is anyone's guess. Embarrassed that his secretary had blown his cover story, he greeted me with a perfunctory handshake and encouraged me to spend time with the permanent exhibition. With that he scurried away.

The house at Friedrichsruh was a gift to Bismarck from a grateful nation after the Franco-Prussian War, and Chancellor Bismarck liked it more than Varzin, his other getaway estate, because it connected him to Berlin in less than two hours by train. The English historian A. J. P. Taylor, however, gives an accurate appraisal of what it was really like. He writes:

> The house at Friedrichsruh was even uglier than the one at Varzin. The original mansion had long disappeared, and its place had been taken by a hotel for week-enders from Hamburg. Bismarck did not even trouble to remove the numbers from the hotel-bedrooms.

The nearby Bismarck Museum has more of the personal effects of Bismarck's life—his boots and his capes, for example, not to mention his pickelhaube helmet, that one with the spike on top that is in many portraits of the Iron Chancellor. The foundation exhibition, where I spent most of my time, sets Bismarck's career in the context of European politics from 1850 to 1890, the years that roughly form the timeline of his political life, although Bismarck was born in 1815 and was first elected to the Prussian parliament in 1847.

In the 1850s he served as Prussia's ambassador in Frankfurt to the German national assembly and later as Prussia's ambassador to Russia in St. Petersburg. Only with the accession of Wilhelm I to the throne of the Prussian monarchy in 1862 was Bismarck appointed prime minister, allowing him to embark on the series of border wars that would unify the various German states into a confederation that would anoint Bismarck as its chancellor in 1867.

The rooms of the exhibition corresponded to the big decisions of Bismarck's political life, so there were cabinets devoted to battles with German liberalism, the war for Schleswig-Holstein, the wars with Austria and France, the cultural battles against the Catholic Church in the 1870s, and the alliance systems that Bismarck constructed to preserve the enlarged German confederation.

In one of the rooms it was possible to push buttons on a map of Europe that illuminated the countries involved in various Bismarckian alliances. Press enough buttons, and at one point every country in Europe is either his friend or enemy. I took pictures—here it was fine to snap away—of the cabinets, plus the declaration of war in 1870.

From the exhibition and the museum, Bismarck looks like a lonely man, as obsessed with nationalism as Clemenceau, even if it means a solitary life largely spent brooding.

Other than his benefactor, patron, and overlord, Kaiser Wilhelm I, Bismarck had few friends—only allies of convenience. Taylor writes: "He had no colleagues, only subordinates." Later it was said, by Edward Crankshaw: "Bismarck has nobody but the king—the elderly monarch who distrusted him and feared him, but found him temporarily indispensable. He succeeded by persuading, cajoling, frightening, bamboozling the king into believing that he [Bismarck] was permanently indispensable."

Bismarck said of himself: "Two things maintain order in my life, my wife and [German parliamentarian Ludwig] Windthorst; the one for love, the other for hate." As chancellor he demanded loyalty to the kaiser, Prussia, and himself, saying at one point: "My ambassadors must wheel in line like soldiers!" Crankshaw concludes: "The tragic Bismarckian paradox was that this great hero of a people who liked to be led was not a leader at all. He was a manipulator." He once said, when asked how he had slept, that he had "spent the night hating."

From his eight years as Prussia's representative in Frankfurt (where sat the government of the Confederation of the Rhine, put together by Napoleon I), Bismarck developed his desire to unify Germany under Prussian leadership, above all other goals. He was jealous of the Austrians, despised Poland for its threat to Prussia, and was always wary of Russia, which he never wanted to challenge.

Biographer Edward Crankshaw describes Bismarck's driving worldview, "which was to harness the spirit of German nationalism to the Prussian cause, specifically by appealing to the material interests of the new bourgeoisie in the lesser states as opposed to the dynastic interests of their princely rulers." It was in Frankfurt that he developed his capacities for scheming. Crankshaw also describes his cunning: "In the four years since his appointment to Frankfurt he had been astonishingly transformed into a diplomatic schemer of extreme subtlety and deviousness, who, unlike most diplomats, had also the makings of a natural master of men."

Almost more than his war with France, the destruction of the Austrian army at Sadowa in 1866 is the most illustrative period piece from the age of Bismarck. In the foundation museum, there is a wing chair that has been sawed in two, to symbolize that the German-speaking world could not have two masters on the same throne. Bismarck made sure that the winner was Prussia, not Austria. Crankshaw summarizes his views on the Confederation:

> Of course Prussia must behave like a loyal member of the Confederation by fulfilling her statutory obligations; but for Austria, primarily a non-German state, to be allowed to dominate the Confederation by sheer weight of numbers, when most of her millions were not Germans at all, was an absurdity. Prussia must champion the spirit of Germany and win to her side the lesser state by appealing to German nationalism.

That attitude led to the war with Austria in 1866, and it explains a letter on display from the liberal jurist Rudolf von Ihering. He writes: "A war has never been instigated with such shamelessness, such an atrocious frivolity—like the one Bismarck tries to provoke against Austria at this moment. The soul is outraged at such a sin against all principles of right and morality."

In his biography of Bismarck, A. J. P. Taylor writes: "In 1866 there was no disguise; Austria fought for her primacy, Prussia for equality. . . . But even Bismarck did not appreciate in 1866 that, by failing to carry the war to a revolutionary conclusion, he had committed himself to the maintenance of Austria as a Great Power." On this point, Crankshaw goes further, arguing that Bismarck, for his own purposes, attacked Austria by inciting nationalist sentiment among its non-German constituent nationalities, which begat the evil genie that later granted the wish of World War I.

Even in his own museum, Bismarck's fingerprints are all over the Franco-Prussian War, from the doctoring of the Ems Dispatch (an exhibit has a picture of French ambassador Vincent Benedetti hectoring Wilhelm I at the baths over the Spanish succession) to the "hard peace" in 1871 that sliced away Alsace and much of Lorraine, including Metz. The actual treaty, with wax seals near the signatures, is in one of the cabinets.

Also on display is a color print of the defeated French emperor sitting dejectedly on that bench in Donchery, while Bismarck sits ramrod-straight with his sword, staring past Napoleon III into what looks like the new European order. Another dramatic painting shows the emperor heading off to his whist imprisonment under the guard of Prussian cuirassiers.

Although none of the exhibits is an apologia for German conduct, the case is made, nevertheless, that Napoleon III was just as responsible for the outbreak of war as was Bismarck, and that the consequence of the war was the desirable goal of German unification. Even historian Geoffrey Wawro makes the case that internal rot in Napoleon's government made war with Prussia a possible panacea:

Gradually this internal crisis in France became a chief cause of the Franco-Prussian War, for Napoleon III, under constant attack in the press, streets, and legislature by 1869–70, began consciously manipulating foreign policy— the hope of "a good war" (*une bonne guerre*) with the Prussians—to restore public faith in the Second Empire.

Wawro describes a February 1870 imperial gala with Napoleon, "'fat, affable, but fragile,' moving ponderously among his guests, speaking slowly as if stricken, drunken officers reeling around the ballroom, prostitutes dancing the can-can, everyone collapsing in a wrack of champagne bottles at dawn."

Taylor puts Bismarck's cynical politics more alongside those of modern leaders, arguing that he was little different from his contemporaries, although much better at picking generals and running the army. "Bismarck aspired to control events," he writes. "He would go to war only 'when all other means were exhausted' and then for a 'a prize worthy of the sacrifices which war demands.' This may shock those who judge by motives instead of by results. But Bismarck's planned wars killed thousands; the just wars of the twentieth century have killed millions."

Also working in Bismarck's favor was his blunt and ironic manner of speech, which left few in doubt either as to his views or what actions might follow. In many respects he is Clemenceau's linguistic predecessor. In 1863, according to Taylor, he said: "The secret in politics? Make a good treaty with Russia." Taylor continues: "Bismarck despised Italy, who had, he said, 'a large appetite and very poor teeth' ... When Italy demanded territorial gains at the 1878 congress of Berlin, he asked: 'What, has she lost another battle?'"

Bismarck disliked overseas expansion, saying (it appears in Taylor): "I am no man for colonies." He said to the French ambassador: "I have had one aim in regard to France for the last fourteen years, since making of peace: to get her to forget the war . . . I want you to forgive Sedan as you have forgiven Waterloo." About war he said: "No one who had looked into the eyes of a man dying on the battlefield will again go lightly into war." In words that might appeal to modern sentiments about the European Union, he observed: "I have always found the word Europe on the lips of those politicians who wanted something from other Powers which they dared not demand in their own names."

As seen from the artifacts of his life that are spread around the two museums, Bismarck strikes me as a toady to those above him and a bully to the rest, a man who could use his physical presence, short temper, and hyperactivity to make sure the world paid court to his vanity. With the kaiser, who relied on him for making daily decisions, Bismarck endlessly played the wounded lover, at crucial times abruptly leaving Berlin for one of his country houses so that Wilhelm could learn firsthand how hard it was to run Prussia and Europe without Bismarck's help. It is the temper tantrum theory of international politics. Henry Kissinger operated much the same way.

Bismarck's approach to the German princes, whom he needed for Greater Prussia, was to divide and rule, and the tactics deployed ranged from war (Schleswig-Holstein) to tariff wars and deception. In foreign affairs, he wanted to believe he was a master diplomatic juggler of competing national interests, but because his mind lacked subtlety and his habits were coarse, he went to war impulsively, largely because it suited his personality to solve problems quickly.

The Franco-Prussian War began from his rewriting of the Ems Dispatch, hardly a considered approach. He is famous for the statement "The important questions of our time are not decided by speeches or majority decision but by iron and blood." The Germany he constructed had more to do with Bismarck vindictively settling past-due accounts—Jena, Tilsit, 1848, Poland—than it did with collective national ideals. On a personal level, I suspect he also loved to manufacture international crises to prove his indispensability, if not to impress Kathy Orlov. Benjamin Disraeli said to Queen Victoria: "His idea of progress is to seize something."

Not everyone in Europe kowtowed to Bismarck, and among those who did not were two Victorias, one the queen of England and the other her daughter, known as Vicky, who was married to Crown Prince Friedrich and mother to Kaiser Wilhelm II. Both found him dishonest, manipulative, scheming, and boorish.

When Queen Victoria's grandson, Wilhelm II, acceded to the Prussian throne in 1888, he initially tolerated his father's loyal retainer, but let him go after one of his outbursts. He complained to Bismarck: "How can I rule without discussing things with the ministers, if you spend a large part of the year at Friedrichsruh?" Crankshaw elaborates the alliance that brought him down:

> But in the end he himself was destroyed, and through the manner of his destruction Vicky had her posthumous revenge; for he was destroyed by her own son, the emperor William II, whom he had set against his mother and encouraged in his excesses, and who went on to

destroy the Germany that Bismarck had created. So ruin came, rather later than Vicky had foreseen, and rather more tortuously, but for the reason she gave: the character of Bismarck.

The English humor magazine *Punch* ran its famous cartoon, "Dropping the Pilot," that shows Bismarck descending the companionway of a ship while Wilhelm II watches him go. The foundation exhibit has a reprint of the cartoon, as well as another showing Wilhelm giving Bismarck, with only his dog to second him, a cold reception. I imagine that he spent that night hating.

Theodor Fontane Chips Away at
the Rock of Bronze
Hamburg

To GET BACK TO HAMBURG, I waited on the Friedrichsruh platform outside the foundation and rode a local train about thirty minutes to the main station. From there, I was catching another train to Amsterdam and then a flight to the U.S., the first time I would be back since my mother had died.

As I had several hours until my Amsterdam train, I decided to walk around Hamburg and, when I got cold, have lunch in a café overlooking the canals that cut through the city. Hamburg was windswept but sunny, more Baltic winter than autumn. I followed my nose around the center, happy to see Hanseatic architecture and to be close to the sea.

Over lunch I started reading *Effi Briest*, a novel by Theodor Fontane, a German writer I had only recently discovered. His life spanned most of the nineteenth century, although he wrote nearly all of his novels in the last twenty years of his life, between 1878 and 1898. When I learned more about Fontane, I discovered that his work often addresses the legacy of the Franco-Prussian War, and that his characters tend to live in large Baltic manor houses—another reason I decided to bring *Effi Briest* with me to Friedrichsruh.

All the important dates in *Effi Briest* correspond to the anniversaries of German victories, such as Sedan or Sadowa, the latter of which the Germans call Königgrätz. Effi is a young, naive girl who leaves her parents' house by the sea to be married to a government official, Baron Innstetten, the local governor who is a rising politician, often summoned to meetings at Varzin (the other Bismarck house) or Friedrichsruh.[4]

Effi is a woman in the mold of Edith Wharton's characters, in that her innocence collides with society's harder intangibles. She feels trapped in her loveless marriage. "Innstetten was good and kind," Fontane writes, "but he was not a lover." He looked at his wife as he might have the furniture, something arranged for his comfort, and he is caught up in a career that has landed him in proximity to Bismarck. Fontane writes: "Innstetten now informed her that he would not be undertaking his trips to Varzin this year: the Prince was going to Friedrichsruh, which he seemed to be increasingly fond of." Innstetten says: "The Catholics, our brothers, whom we must respect while opposing them, have the rock of St. Peter, but we must have the *rocher de bronze*." The "rock of bronze" means Bismarck.

Effi feels "like a prisoner, unable to escape," until the arrival of Major Crampas, a dashing officer with an appetite for vulnerable women. In this case, his tastes focus on Effi, with whom she rides horses and has picnics, sometimes while her husband is away. Inevitably Effi succumbs to the sexual

---

4: To make small talk while reading the newspaper, Innstetten says to his wife: "I'm already resigning myself to handing over the reins to other hands, and Louis Napoleon, well, he was completely wax in the hands of his Roman Catholic wife—or shall we rather say, his Jesuitical wife."

wiles of Crampas, although she is never in love with him—just a young, confused, conflicted woman who most of all misses her childhood. Nevertheless, Innstetten finds some of their letters. Ever the Bismarckian, he kills Crampas in a duel, divorces Effi, and keeps their only child. Effi drifts off to Hamburg to live a life of shame and penury. I thought of her dreary cold-water apartment on my walk around the city.

Toward the end of the novel Effi tries confessing to a minister, in a passage that feels surprisingly modern. "Yes," she says, "I'm really afraid and ashamed of all my lying. But I don't feel ashamed of being guilty, not really, or at any rate, not ashamed enough, and this is what's destroying me, because I am ashamed." He responds: "All that high-falutin' talk about 'God's judgement' is nonsense, of course, and we don't want any of that, yet our own cult of honour is a form of idolatry. But we must submit to it, as long as the idol stands." In this case, the idol is Bismarck.

Like Lily Bart (in Wharton's *The House of Mirth*) or Roberta Alden (in Theodore Dreiser's *An American Tragedy*), Effi is made to bear the weight of her sins, in a society that has built itself on the blood of foreign wars, which among other things have paid for Varzin and Friedrichsruh. Effi is forced to confess: "He was always thinking of his career and nothing more. Honour, honour, honour . . . and then he shot that poor man, whom I didn't even love, and whom I'd forgotten because I didn't love him. It was all just stupidity and then blood and murder. And it's my fault."

Waiting in Amsterdam for the plane to take off for the States, I read the last lines of the novel. Effi has died, of a broken heart and abandonment. Effi's parents are having coffee at their house, reflecting on whether they share any "blame" for her fate. (I can't imagine the Bismarcks having such an introspective conversation, unless it was to blame the help or Kaiser Wilhelm II.) When Effi's mother asks her husband whether they might bear responsibility for the course of Effi's life and her fall, by arranging for her to marry at such a young age, Herr Briest cuts off his distraught wife. "Let it go," he says. "That is *too* big a subject."

Out of the Fog
Last Words

I DID NOT READ THOSE LAST WORDS as personal advice for dealing with my own big subject, the recent loss of my mother. But my bike rides around the contours of the Franco-Prussian War, with side trips to the trenches of the Great War, and to the cloistered worlds of Balzac and Talleyrand, had distracted my mind enough to "let it go."

Worrying about train schedules or tired legs, I would no longer replay the last scenes of my mother's life. Reading Balzac or Flaubert as the train poked along from Tours to Bordeaux made me forget all the meetings with her doctors and how at the end her mind had drifted slowly toward oblivion.

When the rail pass expired, I still had many places in France that I wanted to visit, especially the battlefields of the Hundred Years War (Agincourt and Crécy among them) and more of the Loire Valley. I had enjoyed the two months of speaking French, although I had not picked up any of the dialects that Graham Robb describes in *The Discovery of France*.

I loved coming home from the excursion, feeling tired from all the bike riding, but not worn out from the vigil. As my family suspected, I had compromised on hotels, staying wherever I happened to be when I got tired, and I ate many apples, although I assure you that most came from stores. I had not gone out in the evenings—staying in to write e-mails or listen to podcasts—and my notebooks were incomprehensible at times even to me, as when I would write: "Bismarck, duplex man," and then have to comb through my readings to unearth the quotation from Baudelaire.

Apart from those who extended kindness to me as a stranger—the hotelier in Verdun, for example, or the innkeeper in Orléans—the best friends I made along the way came from my books and readings. I was pleased to have the companionship of Boulanger's biographer, James Harding, with his delightful sense of humor. Balzac can be intense, but no one will ever know a French drawing room as well as he did. I wanted to like Flaubert—the man—more than I did, and only after I was home did I embrace Émile Zola, another bard of Second Empire excess.

From afar, the craggy Clemenceau amused me, although I would imagine that in person he was close to insufferable. I never tired of Philip Guedalla and his engaging after-dinner histories of the Second Empire, Napoleon III, Bazaine, and Pétain, and I wished more of my friends had shared the company of Richard M. Watt. In Hamburg, I sheltered from the wind and cold with Theodor Fontane, a novelist who deserves wider readership. I would love to have had them all to a Franco-Prussian dinner—an instinct I know I inherited from my mother. (She also would have insisted on flowers.)

I came home still undecided about Bismarck, although I lean toward the view that he was a flawed genius, not unlike Napoleon I, who was good for his country but bad for Europe. I developed disdain for General "Black Jack" Pershing, who sent his men over the top in an entrenched landscape that assured their destruction, and now see the American involvement in World War I, as do the Harrieses, as the vanguard down the road to the present-day national security state.

I do savor the image of the hotel numbers on the rooms in Bismarck's house in Friedrichsruh, and the phrase in official French communiqués saying that dignitaries in Paris were often "visiting the president of the Senate." Likewise, I am pleased to have seen Balzac's coffeepot and corrected galleys in Paris, and the inscription in Malancourt about the father who went in search of his missing son around Verdun.

I was not sure, when I got back, that I knew more about France as a nation or a country than when I started. I fear I am little different from those early train travelers on the continent, who "saw much, but learned little." At least I did have engraved in my mind the landscape of that fatal vortex between Metz and Sedan, and I no longer look at a map of France and wonder what lies between Lyon and Tours.

When I got home, I loved to think about my time in the sunshine and on those small roads that twisted through the Argonne, and I shivered when remembering my walk in the cold mist around Biarritz. My favorite cities were Orléans and Bordeaux, and the only thing that had felt dangerous was the night bike ride at breakneck speed across Paris to Gare Austerlitz.

Only with my father, when I arrived back in Princeton, did I recount the day-by-day details. He could never hear enough quotes from Clemenceau or details about the love life of General Boulanger. Others in my life, while happy that I had been "out on the bike in France," didn't jump in with questions when I would say that I had "made it to Sedan."

Next time I set out on my bike, I might leave the computer at home—in many senses of the word, it weighed a lot—and force myself to eat one good meal each day. I also have it in mind to buy a better rain jacket and "under armor" to wick away sweat on the hills toward Gravelotte. But I can't imagine ever moving around France without a bicycle.

I never did count up the miles I rode on the bike or trains, but I did make it to many corners of France. I did not reconcile myself to the Lyon train station—a corner of a foreign field that will never be mine—and I have unpleasant memories of some rudeness from SNCF conductors whenever I botched a TGV reservation or sat in the wrong seat. I still have all the books (dragged home in my saddlebags) from my travels stacked up next to my office chair, fearful that when I return them to their proper place on my shelves the ride will be over.

Even in my imagination, I prefer to be out on the road on what the French in the late nineteenth century liked to call the feedless horse. My own two wheels might have helped me flee dark memories in Princeton, New Jersey, but when that flight from Amsterdam landed in New York, I remembered that I had left the morning fog hanging over Montmédy and found sunshine—of all places—on the fateful road to Sedan.

About the Author

MATTHEW STEVENSON was born in New York City and grew up on Long Island, attending Buckley Country Day School and Friends Academy. His university degrees are from Bucknell and Columbia universities, and he spent a year abroad with the Institute of European Studies in London and Vienna. He moved to Geneva, Switzerland, in 1991. He is a contributing editor to *Harper's Magazine* and host of the syndicated radio program, *The Travel Hour*. He has worked professionally in finance and investing. His essays and reporting have been published in many magazines, including, most recently, in *CounterPunch*. He is married to Constance Fogler, and they have four children: Helen, Laura, Henry, and Charles.